Second Grade Scholar

P9-CEV-983

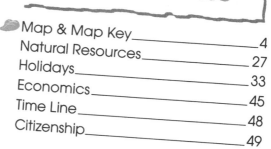

Language Arts

Social Studies

Mathematics

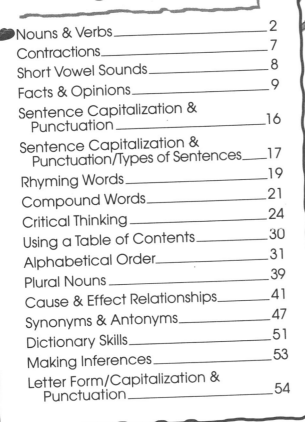

Science

©School Zone Publishing Company

Contents

Let's Go

Mrs. Cone's class is visiting the Green Botanical Gardens today. The words for things the students will see are **nouns**.

workers	squirrels	**flowers**	home
father	**bugs**	trees	**park**

Nouns name people, animals, things, and places.

Read the sentences. Circle the nouns that name people.

1. Our teacher is taking the class to the Gardens.

2. Two parents are coming, too.

3. A guide will talk about different kinds of gardens.

4. All the visitors will have maps to use.

5. Write a sentence about the trip. Circle the nouns.

_____

_____

Try It!

How many nouns about gardens can you and a friend think of in three minutes?

Nouns & Verbs

These words tell what the class will do.

walk   watch   run   **learn**

talk   **laugh**   eat   **sit**

Words that tell what people, animals, and things do are **verbs**.

Read the sentences. Underline the verbs.

6. We're carrying our lunches.

7. Everyone climbs into the bus.

8. The driver starts the bus.

9. We wave good-bye to our friends.

10. Write a sentence about the trip. Underline the verbs.

_____

_____

_____

Word to Know!

A botanical garden is a special garden where plants are shown for visitors to enjoy. Scientists study plants at botanical gardens, too.

Try It!

Choose a story from a magazine. Read the story. Then mark the nouns with a pink marker. Mark the verbs with a yellow marker.

Getting There

A **map** is a picture of a place. This map shows the route from Perry School to Green Botanical Gardens. The **map key** explains the small pictures on the map.

1. Draw the shortest path from the school to the Gardens.

2. How many houses does the bus pass on its way to Green Gardens?

   _____

3. How many grocery stores?

   _____

4. How many gas stations?

   _____

5. Write two other places the bus passes.

   _____

   _____

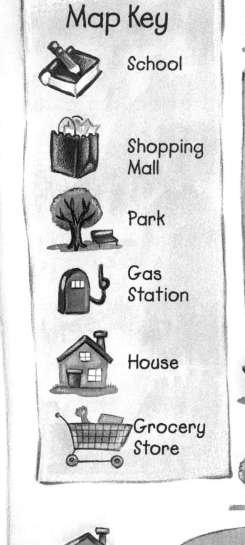

Try It!

Make a map of your neighborhood. Show the streets, the houses, and the other buildings.

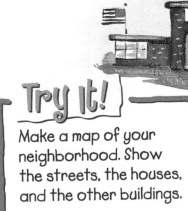

Map & Map Key

5

Ticket Scramble

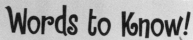

The class is ready to go into the Gardens. But something has happened to their tickets!

Draw lines to match the ticket parts. Then write the sum or difference for each problem.

10-5=

5-4=

7+8=

5+4=

6+6=

8+3=

3-3=

5-2=

Totally True

One botanical garden in Hamilton, Ontario (that's in Canada), has a special 25-acre garden just for children.

9-7=

Try It!

How many addition problems can you think of whose sums are 10? How many subtraction problems can you think of whose differences are 5? Write the problems.

6

Matching Patterns/Addition & Subtraction

Welcome to the Gardens

A **contraction** is a short way to write two words. An apostrophe (') takes the place of the missing letter or letters.

are + not = aren't   what + is = what's   he + will = he'll

The guide is talking to the class about Green Gardens. Write contractions from the box to finish the sentences. Below each sentence, write the words that make the contraction.

I'll   Let's   There's   I'm   We'll   Here's

1. _____ a lot to see at Green Gardens.

   _____ + _____

2. _____ sure the class will enjoy our day.

   _____ + _____

3. _____ what you will see today.

   _____ + _____

4. _____ visit the rainforest and desert areas.

   _____ + _____

5. _____ tell you about the plants there.

   _____ + _____

6. _____ get going!

   _____ + _____

DON'T PICK THE FLOWERS

Totally True
If there were no plants, there would be no life on Earth. The oxygen people and animals breathe comes from plants.

Try It!
Write three contractions you find in a book or magazine story. Then write the two words that make up each contraction.

Contractions

What's in the Tree?

Juan has spotted a colorful bird in a tree.
Would you like to see the bird's colors?

Color the short **a** words **red**.
Color the short **e** words **purple**.
Color the short **i** words green.
Color the short **o** words **brown**.
Color the short **u** words gray.

Turn the page upside down to learn
what kind of bird it is.

Why do storks
stand on one leg?

If they lifted the
other one, they'd
fall over!

Try It!

Write a sentence about a
bird you've seen. Or write
about a made-up bird. Use
one or two of the words in
the picture in your sentence.

painted bunting

Short Vowel Sounds

All About Birds

A **fact** is something that can be proved.
   Birds have feathers.
You can look at a bird or check in a book to find out whether birds have feathers.

An **opinion** is something that someone believes. An opinion can't be proved.
   Birds are beautiful.

Write **fact** or **opinion** after each sentence.

1. Birds have wings.

   _____

2. Birds help plants grow.

   _____

3. Everyone likes the birds at the Gardens.

   _____

4. Birds have bills and claws.

   _____

5. Birds fly too high in the sky.

   _____

6. Cardinals make the Gardens pretty.

   _____

7. Birds make the best pets.

   _____

8. Birds need food and water.

   _____

How is a bird on a wire like a coin?

The head is on one side and the tail is on the other!

Try It!

Read a story about birds. Find at least two facts. Can you find two opinions?

Facts & Opinions

Tweet Code

Add. Then write the letters to find out what the robin is doing.

p
9
+ 7

1.

e
6
+ 5

2.

n
7
+ 6

3.

s
8
+ 7

4.

H
9
+ 8

5.

g
8
+ 4

6.

c
5
+ 4

7.

r
8
+ 6

8.

h
6
+ 4

9.

n
8
+ 5

10.

i
6
+ 2

11.

17	11	,	15		9	10	8	14	16	8	13	12

Try It!

List all the addition facts for 9. Begin with 1 + 8. Then write 2 + 7, 3 + 6, and so on. Pair up the facts that have the same numbers, such as 8 + 1 and 1 + 8. What happens to the sums when you change the order?

Why do birds fly south in the winter?

Because it takes too long to walk!

10

Addition

Weather Watch

What's the temperature? Look at the temperatures at Green Gardens on different days. Write the number of the word that best describes each picture.

1. **hot**   2. warm   3. cold   4. cool

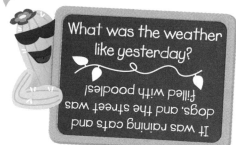

Try It!

Keep a weather log for a week. At about the same time of day, write the temperature and draw a weather symbol in a notebook.

Words to Know!

The study of weather is called **meteorology** (mee-tee-uh-rol-uh-jee). A person who studies weather is called a **meteorologist**.

11

A Clean Scene

Workers and visitors help keep Green Gardens clean. They help **recycle**, or reuse, the trash.

Sort the garbage. On the line under each piece of trash, write the bin in which it goes.

1. _____

2. _____

3. _____ 4. _____ 5. _____ 6. _____

Try It!

Next time you play outdoors, pick up at least one piece of litter and put it where it can be recycled.

Paper   Metal   Plastic   Glass

Recycling

Subtraction Bugs

There are lots of bugs at Green Gardens.

Draw the other half of each bug. Write a subtraction problem that has the same difference on that half. Then color in the rest of the bug.

$$\begin{array}{r} 6 \\ -1 \\ \hline 5 \end{array}$$

$$\begin{array}{r} 9 \\ -4 \\ \hline 5 \end{array}$$

$$\begin{array}{r} 17 \\ -3 \\ \hline \end{array}$$

$$\begin{array}{r} 18 \\ -5 \\ \hline \end{array}$$

$$\begin{array}{r} \\ - \\ \hline \end{array}$$

$$\begin{array}{r} 12 \\ -9 \\ \hline \end{array}$$

$$\begin{array}{r} 18 \\ -4 \\ \hline \end{array}$$

$$\begin{array}{r} \\ - \\ \hline \end{array}$$

$$\begin{array}{r} 9 \\ -7 \\ \hline \end{array}$$

$$\begin{array}{r} 9 \\ -4 \\ \hline \end{array}$$

$$\begin{array}{r} \\ - \\ \hline \end{array}$$

Totally True

Gardeners and fruit growers love ladybugs. Ladybugs eat aphids and scale insects that harm plants.

What kind of insect sleeps most?

A bedbug!

Try It!

Write all the addition facts for 10. Then write matching subtraction facts.

Subtraction

An Ento What?

Maggie knows a lot about insects. She wants to be an entomologist when she grows up.

Look at the creatures. Check the boxes next to the ones that are insects.

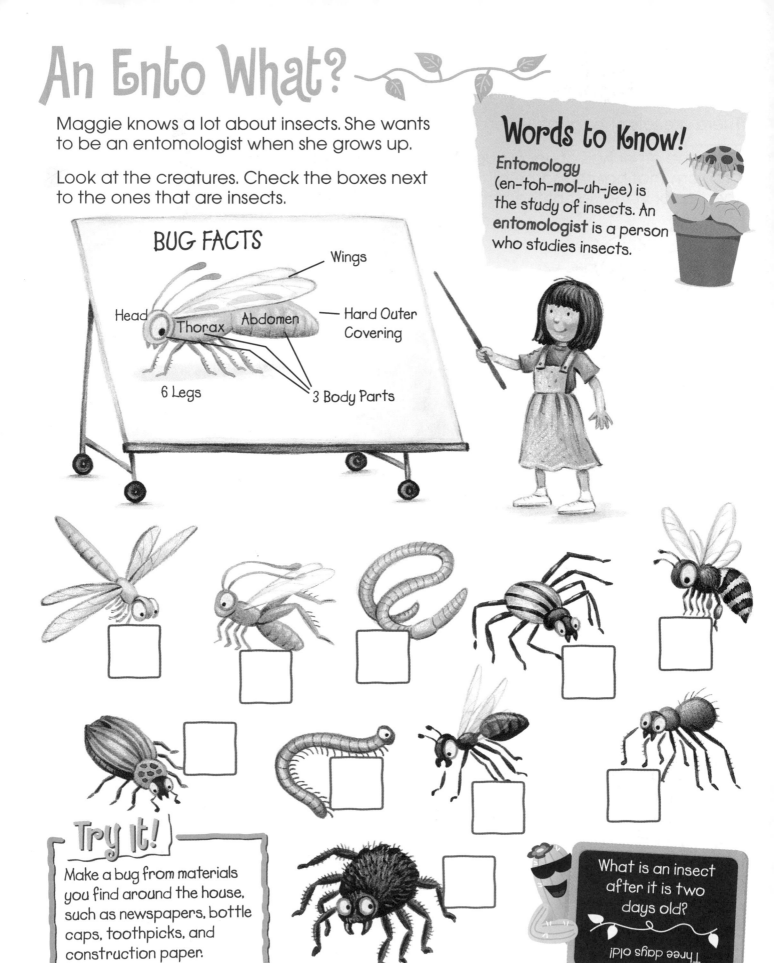

BUG FACTS

Head — Thorax — Abdomen — Wings — Hard Outer Covering — 6 Legs — 3 Body Parts

Try It!

Make a bug from materials you find around the house, such as newspapers, bottle caps, toothpicks, and construction paper.

What is an insect after it is two days old?

Three days old!

Insects

Flutter Numbers

Count by fives. Write the missing numbers in the 100 chart.

5	10		20	25
30	35	40		50
55		65	70	75
	85	90		100

Which number is five after?

25 _____

50 _____

80 _____

Which number is five before?

_____ 30

_____ 65

Start at 5. Connect the dots. Write the missing numbers.

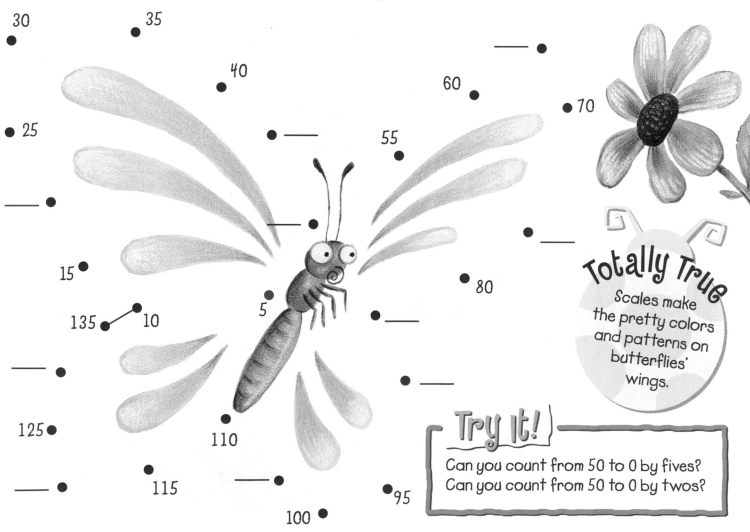

30

35

40

_____

60

_____ 70

25

55

_____

15

135 — 10

5

80

_____

125

_____

110

_____

115

100

95

Totally True
Scales make the pretty colors and patterns on butterflies' wings.

Try It!
Can you count from 50 to 0 by fives?
Can you count from 50 to 0 by twos?

15

Skip Counting by Fives

Butterfly Sentences

A **sentence** is a group of words that tells a complete thought. A sentence begins with a capital letter and ends with a punctuation mark. This is a sentence. It tells a complete thought.

Butterflies like sunshine.

This is not a sentence. It does not tell a complete thought.

begins life as an egg

Use proofreader's marks to correct mistakes. Add words to make sentences. The first sentence is done for you.

Proofreader's Marks

☰ Make a capital.

∧ Add a word.

⊙ Add a period.

insects   butterflies   flowers   ~~begins~~   kinds   fly

1. a̲ butterfly ∧life as an egg⊙ ___begins___

2. butterflies are __ _____

3. there are many __ of butterflies _____

4. __ live all over the world _____

5. they help __ become fruit and seeds _____

6. most butterflies __ during the day _____

Try It!

Draw a picture of a butterfly. Write a sentence to go with your picture.

Sentence Capitalization & Punctuation

Use a period (.) to end a sentence that tells.
Use a question mark (?) to end a sentence that asks.
Use an exclamation mark (!) to end a sentence that shows strong feeling.

Use proofreader's marks to correct the sentences.
Add words from the box to make sentences.

taste   **who**   defend   live   **stink**

7. Some butterflies __ only a week or two _____

8. how can they __ themselves _____

9. some make themselves __ _____

10. others __ bad _____

11. yuck __ _____

12. __ wants to be a butterfly _____

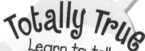

Totally True
Learn to tell a butterfly from a moth.
• Most butterflies fly during the day; moths fly at night.
• Most butterflies have knobs at the end of their feelers; moths don't.
• Most butterflies have thin bodies without hair; moths have fat, furry bodies.
• Most butterflies rest with their wings up; moths rest with their wings out flat.

Try It!
Change an asking sentence from the exercise to a telling sentence. Change a telling sentence to an asking sentence. Write the new sentences.

Types of Sentences

Beehive Addition

Finish the beehives. Add the numbers across and down. An example is done for you.

15	2	17
3	3	6
18	5	23

1.

25	3	
2	4	

2.

5	0	
21	6	

3.

5	14	
4	3	

4.

34	3	
12	5	

5.

6	3	
42	4	

6.

17	21	
2	7	

Try It!

Make some addition bee-hives of your own. Make sure the numbers add up across and down.

18

Garden Rhymes

Words that **rhyme** end with the same sound.
The word **sat** rhymes with **mat**.

Read the sentences about plants. Write the rhyming words.

1. Some plants have lots of spots.

   _____   _____

2. Some trees grow very slow.

   _____   _____

3. Some plants have ants.

   _____   _____

4. Some plants have bugs, and other plants have slugs.

   _____   _____

5. Some leaves blow in the wind as they grow.

   _____   _____

6. Some plants grow tall against a wall.

   _____   _____

Try It!

Play this game with another player. Make two sets of letter cards.

set one

| L | C | M | | B | H | H |
| B | N | | W | H | | R |

set two

| and | ow | ame | ell | eat | ide |
| ap | and | ill | one | iss | un |

Put each set of cards in a jar or bowl. Take turns picking out a card from each set. If the card makes a word, write the word. The first player to make three words wins.

Totally True

Scientists believe there are more than 350,000 kinds of plants. But no one knows exactly how many kinds there are.

Rhyming Words

Leaf Pickup

The class is collecting fallen leaves. Subtract to finish the number wheels on the leaves.

Totally True

The sequoia trees of California are the largest living things in the world. They can grow nearly 300 feet high and as much as 100 feet around.

Try It!

Choose a number wheel. Write the addition facts to match the subtraction facts.

Write the differences.

	17 − 9		16 − 8		17 − 8
1.		2.		3.	

	16 − 9		15 − 8		14 − 9
4.		5.		6.	

20

Subtraction

In the Rainforest Garden

A **compound word** is two words put together to make a new word.

The **butterfly** flew around the garden. **Butterfly** is made of the words **butter** and **fly**.

Read the paragraph. Underline each compound word. Then write the words that make the compound word.

When they got to the greenhouses, the class visited the rainforest area. Everyone looked around. They took their notebooks from their backpacks. Someone began drawing the banana plant. Somebody else asked questions about the plant.

1. _____ + _____

2. _____ + _____

3. _____ + _____

4. _____ + _____

5. _____ + _____

6. _____ + _____

7. _____ + _____

Try It!

Write a sentence about the rainforest. Use at least one compound word in your sentence.

Frog or Toad?

Fill in the blanks with words from the box. Then write the letters on the lily pads to find out what group of animals toads and frogs belong to.

smooth   land   bumpy   water   **plump**   **hind**

1. Frogs have long ___ ___ ___ ___ legs.
      1   4

2. Their skin is ___ ___ ___ ___ ___ ___ and moist.
      8

3. Most frogs live near ___ ___ ___ ___ ___.
            5

4. True toads are ___ ___ ___ ___ ___.
      2

5. Their skin is ___ ___ ___ ___ ___ and dry.
      6   3

6. Most toads live on ___ ___ ___ ___.
                  7

___ ___ ___ ___ ___ ___ ___ ___ ___ ___
 5   3   2   1   4   6   4   5   7   8

Try It!
Make a chart showing how cats and dogs are alike and how they are different. For example, both animals have fur. But dogs bark and cats meow.

Amphibians

Find the Pond

Help the frog find the path to the pond.
Start at 20 and count by 2s.

43	32	26	22	33	36	25	22	20	28
42	40	38	36	34	28	27	24	30	29
44	45	41	35	32	30	28	26	27	28
46	48	50	56	58	60	63	65	67	27
43	42	52	54	51	62	64	59	62	74
49	62	78	91	84	67	66	68	70	72
89	95	92	95	88	86	84	82	75	74
94	96	97	93	90	81	75	80	78	76
89	92	98	91	92	91	89	83	81	79
91	88	90	95	94	96	98	100	99	94

Totally True

A frog uses its long sticky tongue to capture flies and other insects.

Try It!

Circle the tens. Then write the tens in order on a sheet of paper.

Rainforest Stories

Read about Green Gardens' rainforest area. Then answer the questions.

Martin and Lee saw something moving in the grass. They heard a peeping sound. The boys ran to see what was making the noise. The guide walked over. "That's a baby quail," she said.

1. What is a quail?

_____

_____

"This area had too many ants," the guide told us. "Quail like to eat ants. That gave us an idea. Now our problem is solved."

2. What was the problem?

_____

_____

3. How was the problem solved?

_____

_____

Try It!

Describe another way the people at the garden could have solved their ant problem.

Critical Thinking

The guide showed the students some bamboo. Bamboo is a kind of giant grass with a hollow stem. Bamboo can grow more than six inches a day. Some bamboo grow as high as 120 feet. That's taller than 24 men standing on each other's shoulders.

4. Does bamboo grow faster or slower than most plants?

_____

5. What is one big difference between grass in a lawn and bamboo?

_____

In the tropics, or hot places on Earth, some people live in bamboo houses and use bamboo furniture. Their mats, baskets, animal pens, and boats are made from bamboo. Bamboo shades their yards.

6. Sum it up. Why is bamboo so important to people in the tropics?

_____

_____

_____

_____

Totally True

Pandas need bamboo even more than people do. Bamboo is the food they eat for breakfast, lunch, and dinner!

Try It!

Invent some other ways that people could use bamboo. Write two or three ideas, or draw pictures to show your ideas.

Critical Thinking

Buy a Snack

Mrs. Cone and her students are visiting the snack bar.

Circle the number of each coin they need to buy the food. Use the fewest coins you can.

quarter = 25¢

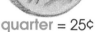
dime = 10¢

nickel = 5¢

penny = 1¢

1. 45¢

2. 85¢

3. 69¢

4. $1.02

5. $1.27
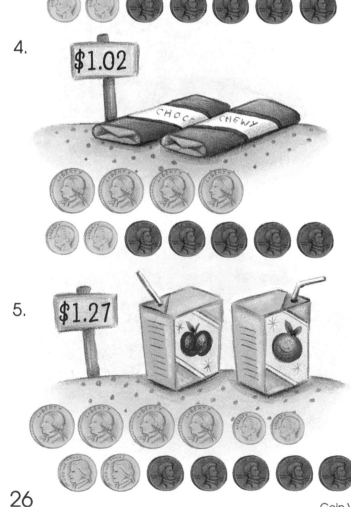

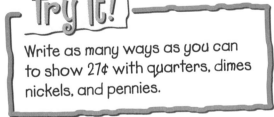
Try It!
Write as many ways as you can to show 27¢ with quarters, dimes nickels, and pennies.

©School Zone Publishing Company

26

Coin Values

Resource Riddles

As the students eat their snacks, the class is talking about nature's useful gifts, or **resources**. They are discussing how to use the earth's natural resources wisely.

Write the resource after each clue.

fish   water   trees   **oil**

1. We use this resource for drinking, cooking, and bathing.

   _____

2. This resource is made into paper.

   _____

3. This resource comes from the ground and is used for fuel.

   _____

4. We can eat this resource.

   _____

5. We can swim in this resource.

   _____

6. We build houses and furniture with this resource.

   _____

Try It!

Write a way to guard, or **conserve**, each of these resources. For example, to conserve trees, you might suggest using both sides of sheets of paper.

Totally True
Wet your toothbrush. Then turn the water off while you brush your teeth. Turn the water on again to rinse. You've just saved as many as nine gallons of water.

Natural Resources

Garden Time

Lots of things are happening at Green Gardens!

Draw the hands on the clocks to show the time of each event. Then write the time.

2:15

Green Botanical Gardens
Schedule, October 5

9:00		Snack Bar Opens
9:40		Garden Talk—Cactuses
10:45		Tour of Greenhouse
11:00		Class—Cooking with Garden Vegetables
12:30		Snack Bar Serves Lunch
1:30		Garden Talk—Taking Pictures of Your Garden
2:15		Cactus Committee Meets
3:05		Tour of Sculpture Garden

_ : _

_ : _

_ : _

_ : _

_ : _

_ : _

Try It!

Keep track of your activities for an evening. Write the time you eat dinner, do your homework, watch TV, and so on.

28

Cactus Subtraction

Find the differences. Draw blossoms on the cactuses for the problems that needed regrouping. Are your answers correct? Check them by adding the answer and the bottom digit. An example is done for you.

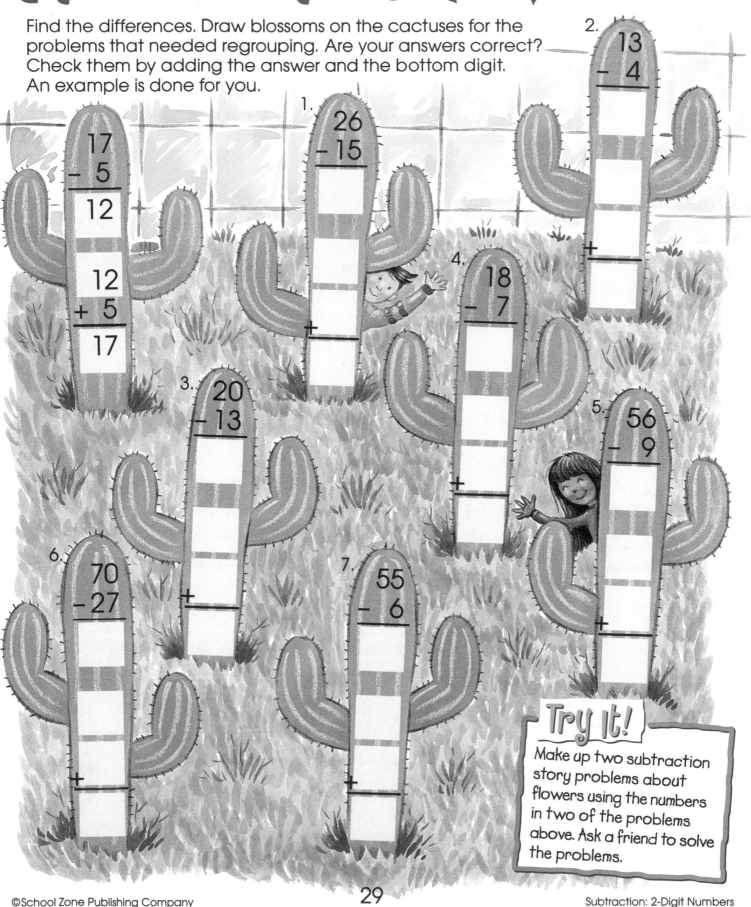

$$\begin{array}{r} 17 \\ -\ 5 \\ \hline 12 \end{array}$$

$$\begin{array}{r} 12 \\ +\ 5 \\ \hline 17 \end{array}$$

1. $\begin{array}{r} 26 \\ -\ 15 \\ \hline \end{array}$

2. $\begin{array}{r} 13 \\ -\ 4 \\ \hline \end{array}$

3. $\begin{array}{r} 20 \\ -\ 13 \\ \hline \end{array}$

4. $\begin{array}{r} 18 \\ -\ 7 \\ \hline \end{array}$

5. $\begin{array}{r} 56 \\ -\ 9 \\ \hline \end{array}$

6. $\begin{array}{r} 70 \\ -\ 27 \\ \hline \end{array}$

7. $\begin{array}{r} 55 \\ -\ 6 \\ \hline \end{array}$

Try It!

Make up two subtraction story problems about flowers using the numbers in two of the problems above. Ask a friend to solve the problems.

29

Subtraction: 2-Digit Numbers

What's in a Book?

Kim and LaTasha want to learn more about cactuses. They choose a book about their subject. They read the contents page to find out what information is in the book.

Contents

1. To which page would you turn to find

   what kind of cactus the girls saw in the greenhouse?

   _____

   the name of the sharp parts of a cactus?

   _____

   how cactuses grow?

   _____

   another book about cactuses?

   _____

   how some cactuses are used in medicines?

   _____

2. What would be a good title for this book?

   _____

Totally True

Cactuses only grow a few inches a year, but they can live a long time. Some cactuses can live as long as 200 years!

Try It!

Go to the library to find books about plants that interest you. Do the books have contents pages? Read the contents pages. Which book would you most like to read? Why?

Put the Book List in Order

Help the Green Gardens librarian. She has a list of new books. The list needs to go in alphabetical order by the title of the book.

Number the books in alphabetical order.

_____ **Mosses and Ferns**
      by Eugenia Charles

_____ **How Plants Grow**
      by M. E. Patinkin

_____ **Amazing Seeds**
      by Janice Carson

_____ **Plant Kingdoms**
      by Alice Addams

_____ **Wildflowers of Michigan**
      by Henry Spinella

_____ **First Seeds, Then Plants**
      by Gary Grove

Totally True

Some plants eat insects. Pitcher plants have tube-shaped leaves that fill with water. Insects fall in and drown. Sticky hairs on the leaves of sundew plants trap insects. Leaves of a Venus's-flytrap snap shut on insects unlucky enough to land on them.

Try It!

Can you teach a younger child how to put words in alphabetical order? You could use flash cards or a stack of books. Show the child what to do if the first letters of two words are the same.

The Garden Calendar

Green Botanical Gardens are open every month of the year. The Gardens are open every week of the year. But the Gardens are closed on a few days.

1. JANUARY   2. FEBRUARY   3. MARCH

4. APRIL   5. MAY   6. JUNE   7. JULY

8. AUGUST   9. SEPTEMBER   10. OCTOBER   11. NOVEMBER   12. DECEMBER

1. What month comes after

   April?_____   September?_____

   December?_____   June?_____

   February?_____   August?_____

2. What month comes before

   October?_____   May?_____

   January?_____   September?_____

   July?_____   March?_____

Try It!

Look at a calendar. Find your birthday. Write the month, date, and day (for example, May 3, Thursday). How long until your birthday?

What do you get when you cross a turkey with an octopus?

Enough drumsticks for Thanksgiving!

It's a Holiday

Green Gardens are closed on special days called **holidays**.

Write the letter to match each holiday to the reason we celebrate it.

A. We celebrate our country's independence.

B. We celebrate a leader who wanted all people to be treated fairly.

C. We celebrate the discovery of America.

D. We celebrate the new year.

E. We celebrate special friends.

What do you call a card from an animal with prickly spines?

A porcupine valentine!

☐ Martin Luther King Day, January 20

☐ Columbus Day, Second Monday in October

☐ Valentine's Day, February 14

☐ New Year's Day, January 1

Try It!

Look at a calendar. On a separate piece of paper, answer these questions.
• Which holiday will you celebrate next?
• What is your favorite holiday?
• Why do you like it best?

☐ Independence Day, July 4

Holidays

What's Where in the Gardens

The **perimeter** is the distance around a figure. The perimeter is measured in units like this:

1 unit = •——½"——•.

1. Find the perimeters of the different parts of the Garden. Write them on the blanks.

2. Which area is the biggest?

_____

Now answer the questions about the shapes.

rectangle **square**
triangle

3. What is the shape of the outdoor cafe?

_____

4. What is the shape of the orchard?

_____

5. What is the shape of the rose garden?

_____

How can you tell which end of the worm is the head?

Tickle it and see which end laughs!

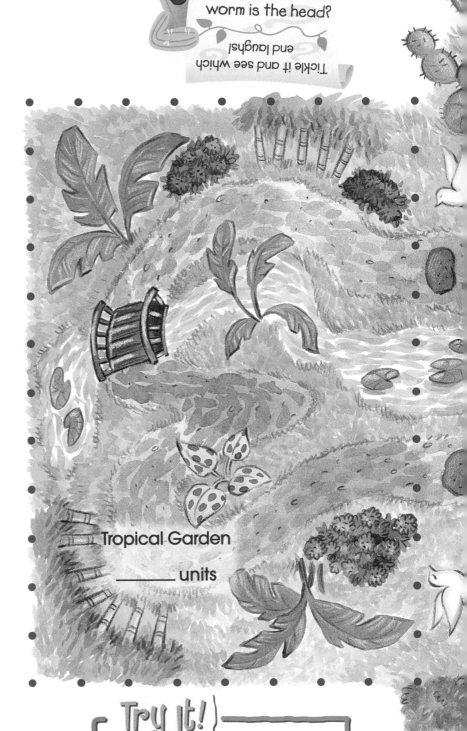

Tropical Garden

_____ units

Word to Know!

A mile is 5,280 feet. It takes about 20 minutes to walk a mile.

Try It!

Measure the perimeter of some of the rooms in your house. Make a list of your results.

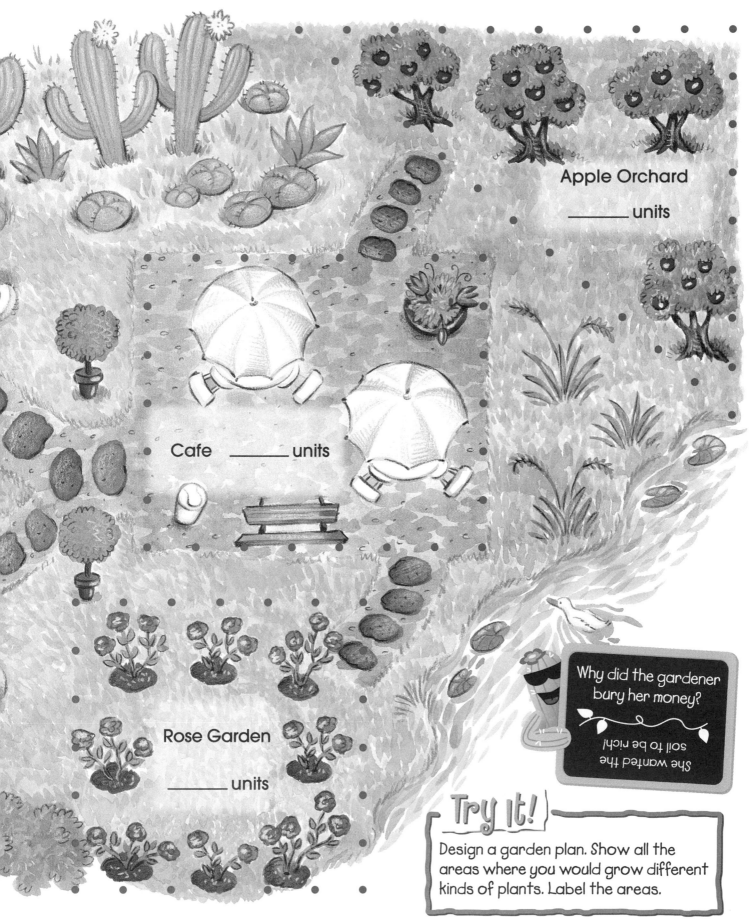

Apple Orchard

_____ units

Cafe _____ units

Rose Garden

_____ units

Why did the gardener bury her money?

She wanted the soil to be rich!

Try It!

Design a garden plan. Show all the areas where you would grow different kinds of plants. Label the areas.

Geometry: Perimeter/Geometric Shapes

Solid, Liquid, or Gas?

Think about it. Everything you see is solid (like rocks), liquid (like milk), or gas (like steam). Most things have only one form—solid, liquid, or gas. Some things can take more than one form.

Look at the picture of Green Gardens. Write solid, liquid, or gas on the lines.

Try It!

Try these experiments with matter.

1. Pour water from a faucet into a glass. What form does the water take?

2. Put some water in the freezer. What form does the water take?

3. Ask a grown-up to help you boil some water. What do you see above the boiling water?

How many forms can water take?

Fractions in the Kitchen

Cooks at the Green Gardens restaurant kitchens use fractions to follow recipes. Look at the fractions in the measuring cups.

½ cup

⅓ cup

¾ cup

Write the fraction of each circle or square that is blue.

1. _____

2. _____

3. _____

4. _____

Write the fraction of each rectangle that is green.

5. _____

6. _____

7. _____

Read each fraction of a cup. Color in the amount.

²/₄ cup

²/₃ cup

¹/₃ cup

⁴/₄ cup

¹/₄ cup

Try It!

You need a measuring cup, a clear glass, and rice or beans for this activity. Fill the measuring cup to the marks that show 1/4, 1/3, and 3/4. Then use an unmarked glass to estimate 1/4, 1/3, and 3/4 full.

Totally True

There are more than 300,000 restaurants in the U.S. They serve over 130 million meals every day!

37

Fractions

A Plant Is Growing!

Some seeds grow into new plants. A seed bursts through its coat. Then roots grow down into the soil. A shoot grows up toward the sunlight. Leaves grow from the shoot. As the plant gets bigger, buds appear. The buds open up into blossoms.

A flowering plant is growing, but the order is mixed up. Number the pictures from 1 to 6 in the correct order.

Word to Know!
When seeds **germinate**, they burst through their coats and grow roots and shoots.

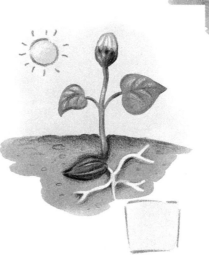

Try It!
Germinate lima bean seeds from packaged seeds. Wrap wet paper towels around the inside of a jar. Add water. Put the seeds between the inside of a jar and the paper towels. Leave the jar on a windowsill. Make sure the paper towels stay wet. In about a week, your lima bean seeds should germinate.

38

Lots of Seeds

You add **s** to many nouns to make them name more than one. Write these nouns in the sentences. Add **s**.

seed   coconut   dandelion   **tree**

1. Most plants grow from _____.

2. The soft white fluff on _____ is their seeds.

3. Some seeds become huge _____.

4. Did you know that _____ are seeds?

You add **es** to nouns and other words that end in **s**, **x**, **ch**, and **sh** to name more than one. Write these words in the sentences. Add **es**.

wish   teach   **class**   bus

5. Green Gardens has _____ about plants.

6. Students take _____ to the Gardens.

7. My mother _____ she could come.

8. She _____ at our school.

 **Try It!**

Read a story about seeds in a magazine or book. After you enjoy the story, see if you can remember two or three nouns from the story that name one. Can you remember a couple of nouns that name more than one?

Living Riddles

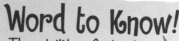

Plants can be tricky. Here are some ways they defend themselves.

Solve the riddles. Write the name of each plant. Use the pictures and words if you need help.

1. Ouch! Watch out for my spines.

_____

2. I'm not poison ivy, but I'll make you itch!

_____

3. People eat my fruit, but insects hate my citrus oil.

_____

4. Prickles keep insects away from me.

_____

5. Cut my blossoms carefully, or you'll prick your finger.

_____

Thistle

Rose

Cactus

Try It!

Look at a bird, squirrel, or other animal that lives near your house. How does the animal protect itself?

Orange

Poison Oak

Garden Happenings

When rain falls in a garden, plants grow. Rain **causes** the plants to grow. The **effect** of the rain is the growing plants. Look for why things happen when you read. This will help you make sense of your reading.

Read each sentence. Write what is likely to happen, or the effect.

1. Mrs. Cone's class is hungry. Effect:

_____

_____

3. All of a sudden, the temperature at the Gardens drops. Effect:

_____

_____

2. A very strong wind comes up. Effect:

_____

_____

Fill in each sentence. Write what made things happen, or the cause.

4. _____

_____ ,

so people take off their jackets.

5. _____

_____ ,

so Mrs. Cone looks for him.

6. _____

_____ ,

and each student has a taste of star fruit.

Try It!
The next time you read a story, see how many causes and effects you can find. Write two or three examples.

At the Garden Store

Practice measuring. Use a ruler or trace the one on page 43 onto another sheet of paper. Cut out your paper ruler.

Guess how many inches long each item is. Then measure with your ruler to see how close your estimate was.

on page 43

What has a foot on each side and one in the middle?

A yardstick!

Estimate   Actual

Estimate   Actual

Estimate   Actual

Estimate   Actual

Words to Know!

There are 12 inches in a **foot**. There are 3 feet in a **yard**.

Try It!

Practice measuring some large things in your bedroom. How many feet long is your bed? your desk?

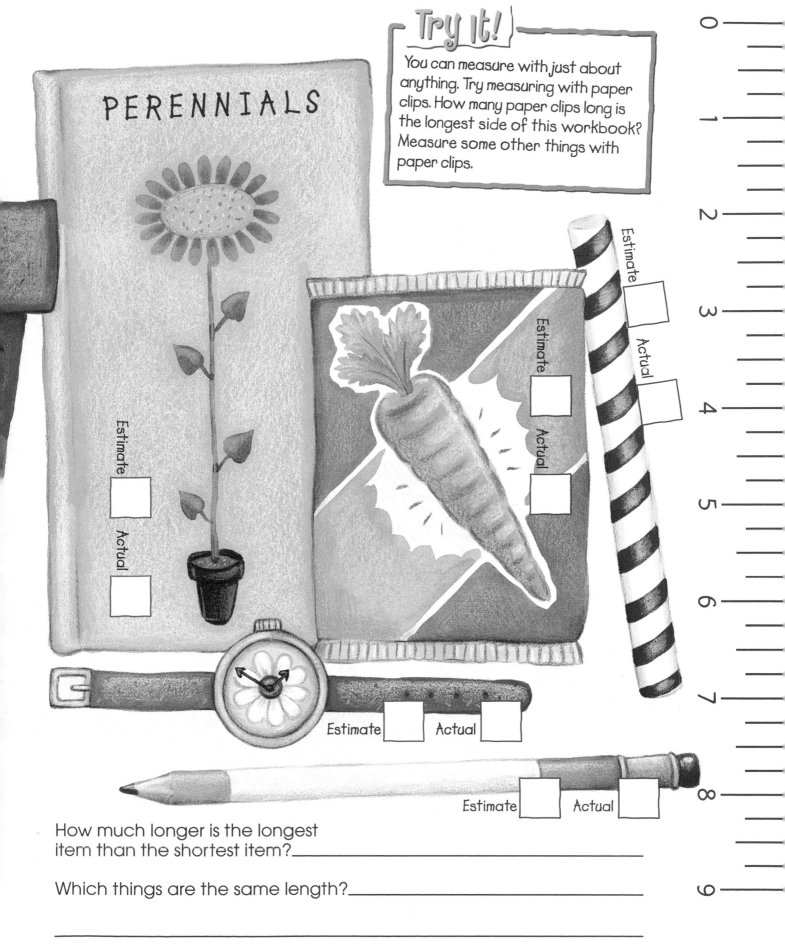

Try It!

You can measure with just about anything. Try measuring with paper clips. How many paper clips long is the longest side of this workbook? Measure some other things with paper clips.

PERENNIALS

Estimate

Actual

Estimate

Actual

Estimate

Actual

Estimate

Actual

Estimate

Actual

Estimate

Actual

0 1 2 3 4 5 6 7 8 9

How much longer is the longest item than the shortest item?_____

Which things are the same length?_____

What's it For?

The scientists at Green Gardens use many different kinds of tools. Here are some of them.

Scale

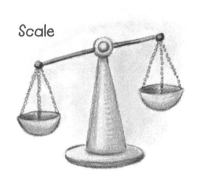

Thermometer

Tweezers

Measuring Cup

Trowel

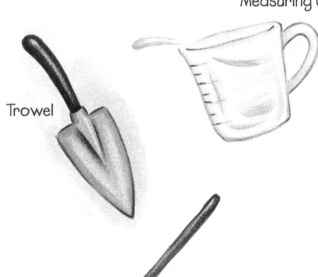

Tape Measure

Rake

1. If you want to find out the temperature, which would you use?

_____

2. If you want to pick up some tiny seeds, which would you use?

_____

3. If you want to plant a seedling, which would you use?

_____

4. If you want to measure how tall a plant is, which would you use?

_____

Try it!

What tools do gardeners use? Make a list or draw some tools and label them.

Producers and Consumers

Producers grow, make, or build things. **Consumers** buy or use **products**, the things that producers make. Every country needs producers to make things and consumers to buy them.

Look at the scenes from the garden.
Write **producer** or **consumer** on the lines.

1. _____

3. _____

4. _____

2. _____

5. _____

Garden Code

Do you remember how to regroup when you add? Here's an example. The answer is 21.

$$\begin{array}{r}\overset{1}{1}4 \\ +\ 7 \\ \hline 1 \end{array} \quad \begin{array}{r} ^{\text{tens}}14 \\ +\ 7 \\ \hline 21 \end{array}$$

🍃 Add the numbers. Then use the code to learn a plant fact that may surprise you.

LL	VA	OR	NI
29	18	15	17
+ 3	+ 5	+ 5	+ 9

A	S	CE	O
32	16	10	17
+ 8	+ 6	+14	+ 8

DU	CH	PR	ID
15	17	15	33
+16	+24	+15	+17

___ ___ ___ ___
20 41 50 22

___ ___ ___ ___
30 25 31 24

___ ___ ___ ___ .
23 26 32 40

Try It!

Think of a math code of your own. Write a message using your code. Ask a friend to figure out your message.

Addition: 2-Digit Numbers

Bunches of Flowers

Some words have the same or nearly the same meaning. **Smile** and **grin** mean almost the same thing.

Draw lines to connect the pairs of words on the cornflowers that have the same or nearly the same meanings.

stop

mistake

ill

like

start

go

sick

enjoy

error

leave

end

begin

Other words have opposite meanings. **Begin** is the opposite of **end**.

Draw lines to connect the pairs of words on the daisies that have opposite meanings.

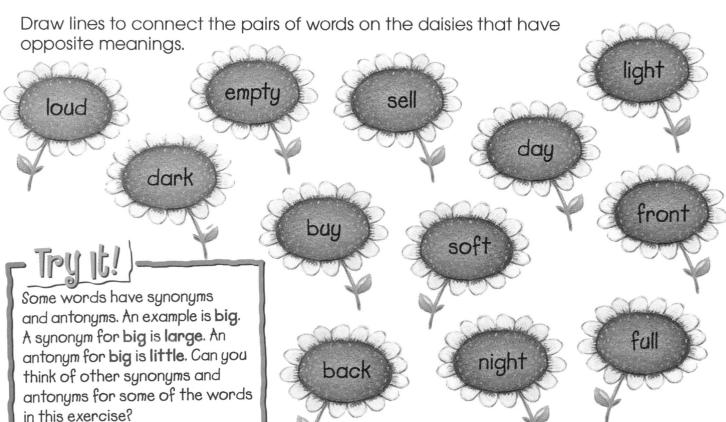

loud

empty

sell

light

dark

day

buy

soft

front

back

night

full

Try It!

Some words have synonyms and antonyms. An example is **big**. A synonym for **big** is **large**. An antonym for **big** is **little**. Can you think of other synonyms and antonyms for some of the words in this exercise?

Synonyms and Antonyms

Time Line

A time line is a good way to show when things happened. A time line can show a day, a month, a year, or longer.

Here is a time line of the children's visit to Green Botanical Gardens.

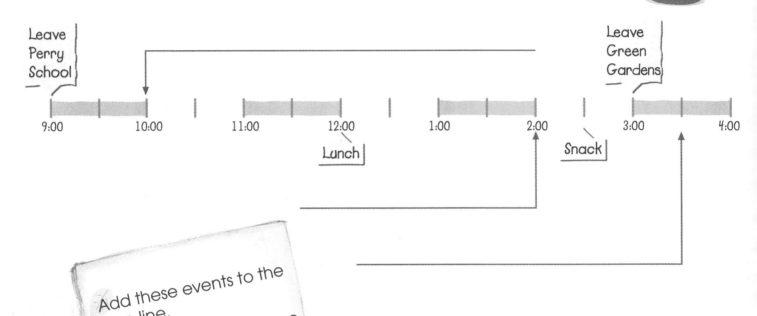

Leave Perry School

Leave Green Gardens

9:00 10:00 11:00 12:00 1:00 2:00 3:00 4:00

Lunch

Snack

Add these events to the time line.

• Tour Greenhouses 10:00

• Visit Library 2:00

• Arrive at School 3:30

Try It!

Make a time line. You can show a day or week in your life. Or you can show the most important things that have happened to you since you were born.

Be a Good Citizen

A good citizen thinks of other people.

Read the descriptions. Write **yes** if a good citizen does this. Write **no** if a good citizen does not do this.

Word to Know!

A **citizen** is a person who lives in a particular town or country.

1. helps others _____

2. writes on library books _____

3. drops trash everywhere _____

4. obeys traffic signs _____

5. runs in school hallways _____

6. follows classroom rules _____

7. Write one other thing you can do to be a good citizen.

_____

_____

Try It!

Add to the list. Describe what makes a good citizen at school.

49

Citizenship

Garden Books

Green Gardens' library has many interesting books for children.

Study the graph. Then answer the questions.

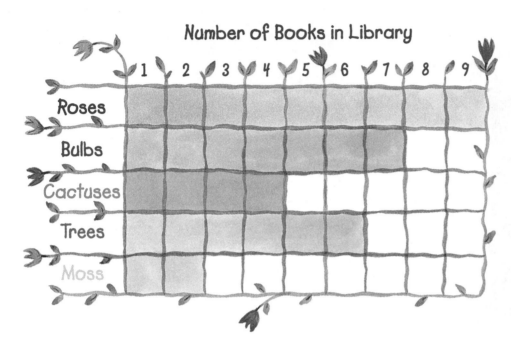

Number of Books in Library

	1	2	3	4	5	6	7	8	9
Roses									
Bulbs									
Cactuses									
Trees									
Moss									

1. How many books are about roses? _____

2. How many books are about trees? _____

3. How many more books are about bulbs
   than about trees?

   _____ ☐ _____ = _____

4. How many more books are about roses
   than about moss?

   _____ ☐ _____ = _____

5. Look at the books about roses and the
   ones about bulbs. How many in all?

   _____ ☐ _____ = _____

Try It!

Find 20 books. They can be from home
or from the library. Sort the books
into groups, for example animal books
and sports books. Then make a chart
or graph that shows how many books
are in each group.

50

Graphing

Wonderful Words

Some words have more than one meaning.
A dictionary numbers each meaning.

Read the definition of **plant**.

> **plant** 1. any living thing that can make its own food from sunlight, air, and water. 2. to put in the ground and grow.

Read each sentence. Write the number of the correct meaning.

a. Where should we plant the rose bush?_____

b. The plant needs water. _____

Read the definition of **bulb**.

> **bulb** 1. a hollow glass light that glows when electricity is turned on. 2. a round bud or stem that you plant in the ground.

Read each sentence. Write the number of the correct meaning.

c. Oh, no! I think the bulb burned out. _____

d. Plant the tulip bulb in the garden._____

Which trees clap?

Palms!

Try It!

When you come to a word you don't know in your reading, don't give up. You can skip the word and try to figure it out from the sentences that follow. You can ask someone what the word means, or you can look up the word in a dictionary. If the word doesn't seem very important, you can ignore it!

Garden Math Puzzle

Solve the problems. Write the answers in the puzzle.

Across

A. 12 more than 10

B. 90, 95, 100, ____

C. $14 + 15 =$ ____

D. $8 + 9 =$ ____

E. $19 - 7 =$ ____

F. 3, 6, 9, ____

G. $120 - 15 =$ ____

H. 2 tens, 8 ones

I. 50¢ + 35¢ = ____

J. $29 - 13 =$ ____

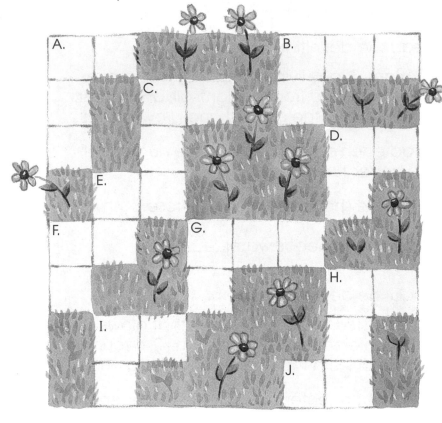

Down

A. $284 + 12 =$ ____

B. $27 - 8 =$ ____

C. 2 hundreds, 2 tens, 2 ones

D. 5, 10, ____

E. one dozen

F. $2 \times 9 =$ ____

G. $3 \times 5 =$ ____

H. 2 hundreds, 3 tens, 6 ones

I. $1.00 - $.15 = ____

Try It!

Write all the numbers used in the puzzle on a sheet of paper. Put them in order from least to greatest.

What's the Problem?

Read the paragraphs. Answer the questions.

1. The class went to the gift shop. Reggie picked out a postcard to buy. He reached into his pocket for money to pay for it. Reggie looked surprised.

   Why do you think Reggie looked surprised?

   _____

   _____

   _____

2. Misty bought her mother a glass bird. When her mother opened the gift, Misty looked sad.

   Why do you think she looked sad?

   _____

   _____

   _____

3. Jill lost her purse. A call came for her from the lost-and-found desk. After Jill answered the phone, she looked happy.

   Why do you think she looked happy?

   _____

   _____

   _____

Totally True

The sap of a tree carries water and food from one part of the tree to another. Maple syrup is made from the sap of the maple tree. But since people don't take too much, they don't hurt the tree when they take the sap.

Try It!

The next time you watch a TV show, choose a character. Try to figure out why the character acts as he or she does. Do you know for sure, or do you have to guess?

Making Inferences

Thanks, Green Gardens

Mrs. Cone's class is sending a thank-you note to Green Gardens.

1. To whom is the letter written?

   _____

2. What is the closing?

   _____

3. Who wrote the letter?

   _____

Write a letter to a friend about a trip you have taken. Look at the letter above to help you.

Date

October 5, 2002

Greeting

Dear Ms. Jones,

Body

Thank you very much for letting us visit Green Gardens. We enjoyed learning about plants in the indoor and out-door gardens. We had fun collecting different kinds of leaves. We especially loved watching the baby quail run around.

Best wishes, **Closing**

Mrs. Cone's class

Signature

Second Grade Summer Scholar

Signs of the Seasons

Signs of the season happen in nature.
Some signs are made by what people do.
Write Spring, Summer, Fall, or Winter under the correct picture.

1. _____

2. _____

3. _____

4. _____

Summer Days

Many words describe summer weather.
Circle the words in the puzzle.

HOT
WET
WINDY
SUNNY
DAMP
BREEZY
DRIZZLY
DRY
RAINY
HUMID

```
H O S U N N Y T D
O M I N Y S D N R
T H U M I D N D I
R M A R A Z O R Z
B T R A I N Y Y Z
R W M A F D E U L
E I O D E Y D T Y
E N F A J P M K H
Z D A M K G T M D
Y Y D P O B W E T
```

Write four words that describe
a good day to go to the beach.

_____   _____

_____   _____

_____   _____

_____   _____

Summer Weather

Time in a Line

A time line is a good way to show the order in which things happen.

The top time line shows the seasons.
The bottom time line shows the months of the year.

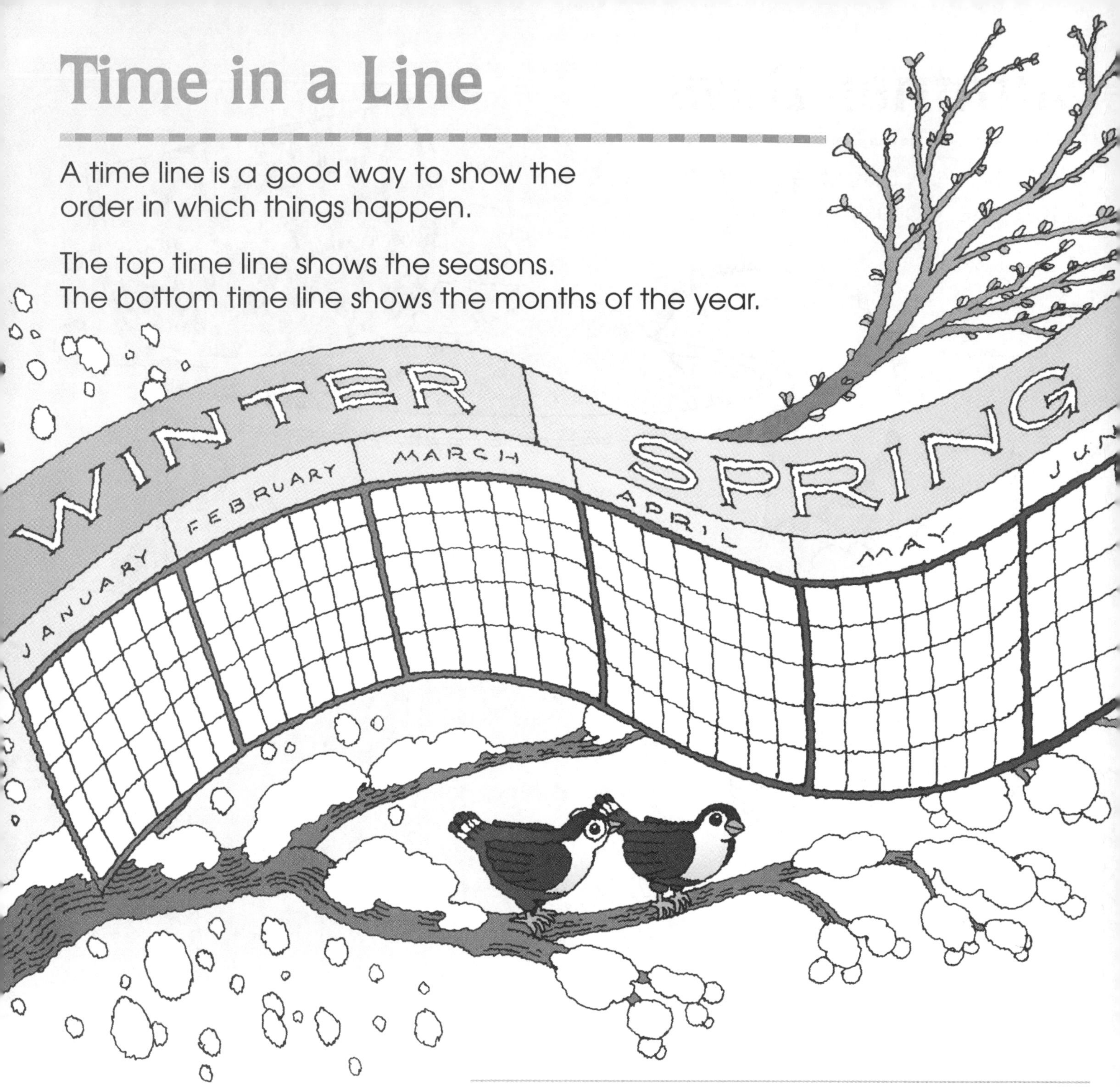

WINTER

SPRING

JANUARY

FEBRUARY

MARCH

APRIL

MAY

JUN

1. January is in what season? _____

2. July is in what season? _____

3. Name a fall month. _____

Calendar

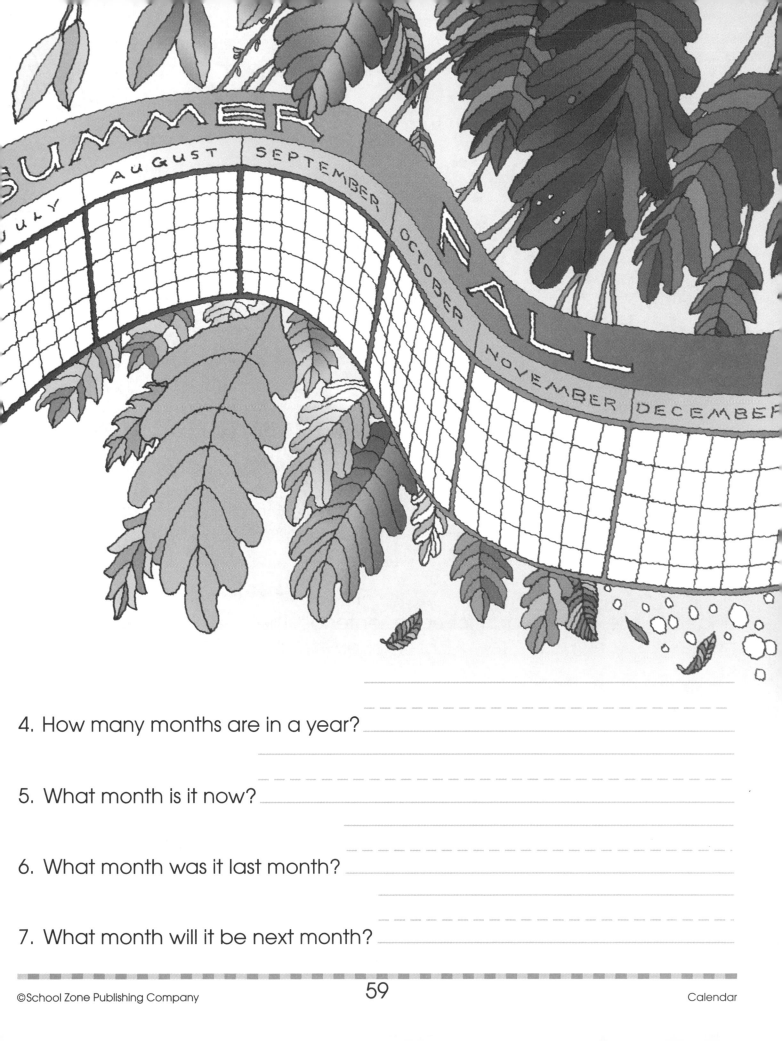

4. How many months are in a year? _____

5. What month is it now? _____

6. What month was it last month? _____

7. What month will it be next month? _____

A Summer Garden

This picture shows a garden in summer.

- A sentence has a **naming part**. The naming part tells who or what the sentence is about.

- The **family** is in the garden. **Who**
- **Flowers** are in bloom. **What**

Underline the naming part for each sentence. Then tell if it names **who** or **what**. Write **who** or **what** on the line.

1. Father picks some tomatoes.

2. Mother waters the flowers.

3. The corn grows tall.

4. The carrots are big.

Sentence Naming Part

Time to Pick

Some things in the garden are ready to pick.

Draw a line from each word to the basket where it belongs.

| tulips | melon | corn | grapes |
| peppers | beans | roses | cherries | lilacs |

Fruit

Vegetables

Flowers

Circle the three things in each group that are alike.

1. carrot   orange   bean   corn

2. hose   rake   shovel   plant

3. leaf   green   stem   root

4. lake   pond   hill   river

5. moon   day   month   year

6. fly   worm   bee   mosquito

Classification

Summer Foods Are Delicious

In summer, many plants grow fast. Most plants make their own food. They need air, sunlight, and water.

Fruit is the part of a plant that contains the seeds. Some plant seeds dot the outside of the fruit.

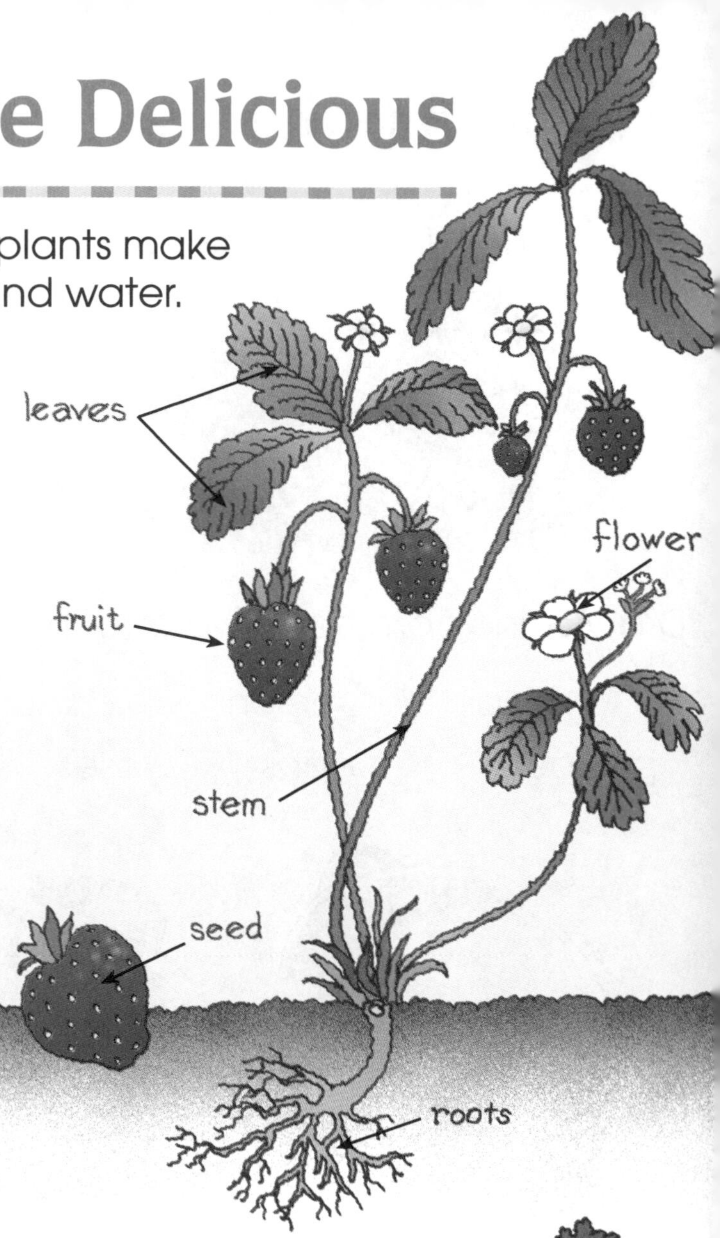

leaves

flower

fruit

stem

seed

roots

People eat different parts of plants.
Write the name of the plant part we eat.

1. People eat the _____ of some plants.

2. People eat the _____ of some plants.

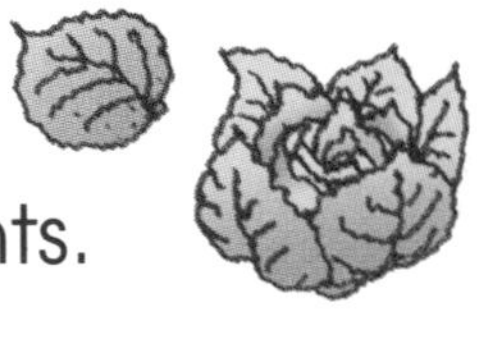

3. People eat the _____ of some plants.

Draw your favorite food from a plant. What part is it?

4. People eat the _____ of some plants.

5. People eat the _____ of some plants.

6. People eat the _____ of some plants.

Let's Go for a Swim!

These words name things you see at the beach.

girls   book   ball

baby   rocks   Waves

Naming words are called nouns. A **noun** names a person, an animal, a place, or a thing.

Write a noun from the box to finish each sentence.

1. Some boys and _____ are swimming.

2. A big red _____ floats in the water.

3. A woman is reading a _____ .

4. A blue and white umbrella shades a _____ .

5. _____ splash over the _____ .

Nouns

Write two sentences about the beach.
Underline the nouns.

_____

- -

_____

- -

_____

- -

_____

Circle three nouns in each row.
One word is not a noun.

6. pail   snail   fail   tail

7. shell   bell   well   tell

Nouns

A Day at the Beach

A **sentence** is a group of words that tells a complete thought. A sentence begins with a capital letter. A sentence ends with a punctuation mark.

Write a sentence with each group of words. Write them in an order that makes sense.

1. sand Amy in plays the

2. a find seashell Patty Does

3. in Peter pail his sand puts

4. water Brr! cold The is

5. caught ball the Rex

Picnic at the Beach

Add or subtract to find the answer to each story problem.

1. Uncle Jim brought 12 cans of juice. He drank 6. How many does he have left?

    _____ − _____ = _____ cans of juice

2. There are 15 eggs on a plate. If people eat 7 of them, how many will be left?

    _____ − _____ = _____ eggs

3. Mother cooked 13 hot dogs. Then she cooked 5 more hot dogs. How many did she cook?

    _____ + _____ = _____ hot dogs

4. Aunt Mary brought cookies. Eight cookies are on a plate. Eight more are in the box. How many cookies did Aunt Mary bring?

    _____ + _____ = _____ cookies

5. Thirteen people want watermelon. Father cut 6 slices. How many more does he need to cut?

    _____ − _____ = _____ slices

Addition/Subtraction Story Problems

Beach Towels

Each towel has a different design.
How many parts of the whole are colored?
Circle the correct fraction.

1 part shaded
2 parts in all
1/2

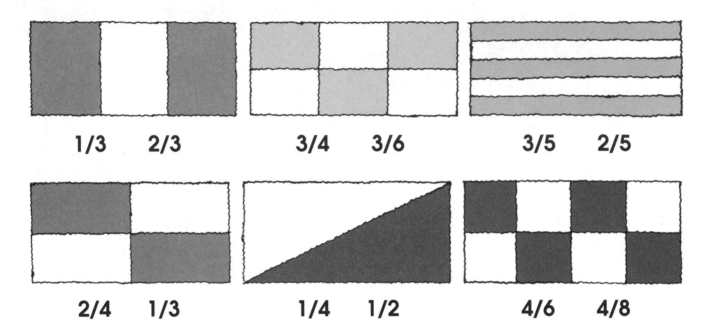

1/3   2/3   **3/4   3/6**   **3/5   2/5**

2/4   1/3   **1/4   1/2**   **4/6   4/8**

Color to show the fraction.

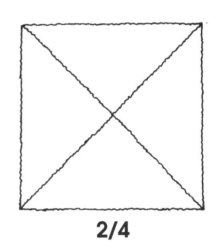

2/3   **2/4**

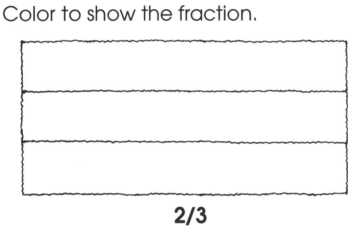

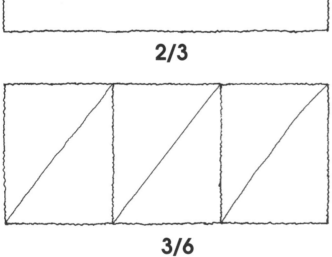

3/6   **1/3**

Fractions

Whirling Wheels

Add to finish these number wheels.

Subtract to finish these number wheels.

One Hundred Years Ago

Even 100 years ago, people liked the beach. There are now new things to do at the beach.

Circle three things that are new. ✓ three that people did 100 years ago.

Past & Present

Yesterday and Today

Some work has also changed over time. Some has stayed the same. Draw a line to show how work was once done to how it has changed.

What has stayed the same? ✔ the picture.

100 Years Ago	**Today**

71

Fun Months

Proper nouns begin with a capital letter. The months of the year are proper nouns. Read the clues. Write the name of the month.

1. Valentine's Day

2. Fourth of _____

3. Halloween

4. Christmas

5. Your birthday

Days of the week and names of people and places are also proper nouns. Write the proper nouns.

6. Your favorite name

7. Your favorite day of the week

8. Your favorite city or town

A Parade of Adjectives!

Every year on July 4, there is a parade.
These words describe things in the parade.

Six	loud	shiny	tall
pretty	blue	furry	big

Describing words are called **adjectives**. Adjectives describe nouns. Some adjectives tell how things sound, look, and feel. Write an adjective from the box to finish each sentence.

1. A _____ man in a _____ hat leads the parade.

2. _____ musicians march in their _____ uniforms.

3. A _____ girl plays a _____ horn.

4. The _____ drum makes a _____ sound.

High, Higher, Highest

Write the adjective using **er** or **est**.

1. Debby's baton is (high) than Gail's.

2. Perri's baton is the (high) of all three.

3. The (smooth) twirler on the team is Gail.

4. Debby is a (fast) twirler than Perri.

5. Perri is (old) than Debby.

6. Gail is the (young) of all.

- Add **er** to some adjectives to compare two people, animals, places, or things.

- Add **est** to some adjectives to compare more than two nouns.

Forming Adjectives

Compound Words

Sometimes two words are joined together to make a new word.
  The parade lasted all **afternoon**.
  after + noon = afternoon
A word that is made by joining two words is a **compound word**.

Read the story. Underline each compound word. Then write
the two words that make the compound word.

Tracy and her family went downtown to watch the parade.
They found a good spot between the playground and the
schoolhouse. It was a hot day. They were standing outside in
the sun for a long time. Luckily, the fireworks were at nighttime.
So Tracy and her family cooled off in the evening.

1. _____ + _____

2. _____ + _____

3. _____ + _____

4. _____ + _____

5. _____ + _____

6. _____ + _____

Compound Words

Dress for the Weather

Weather changes from day to day. Weather also changes with the seasons.

A **thermometer** measures temperature. The warmer the weather, the higher the liquid in a thermometer rises. Temperature is measured in degrees. These thermometers go up and down by two-degree steps from -10°.

- **Weather** is made up of temperature, precipitation, and wind speed.
- **Temperature** tells how hot or cold the air is.
- **Precipitation** is water in the form of rain, snow, sleet, or hail.
- **Wind** is moving air.

This thermometer says 32°, the temperature at which water freezes. It's cold!

This thermometer says 76°. Shorts can be worn on this warm day.

This thermometer says 56°. It's cool today. A sweater feels good.

Weather Definitions

Summer, Fall, Winter, and Spring

Read the thermometers. Write each temperature in the box. Then draw a line from each child to the temperature for which he or she is dressed.

Reading Thermometers

What Makes Weather?

Write weather words to fill in the puzzle.

Across

1. What we wear depends on the _____ .

6. Rain, snow, and hail are kinds of _____ .

Down

2. The push of air on the earth is _____ .

3. _____ is what happens when water turns to water vapor.

4. Cold air can't hold as much _____ as warm air can.

5. Moving air is _____ .

wind
water
air pressure
precipitation
weather
Evaporation

Weather Crossword

Lemonade for Sale!

25¢

20¢

You have made some lemonade and cookies.
You sell them to people in your neighborhood.
Write the correct answer to each problem.

1. Tony buys 1 ⬚ and 1 🍪 .

   What does he owe? _____ ¢ + _____ ¢ = _____ ¢

2. He gives you 2 quarters.
   How much change
   should you give back? _____ ¢ − _____ ¢ = _____ ¢

3. Jeanne buys 1 ⬚ and 2 🍪🍪 s.

   What does she owe? _____ ¢ + _____ ¢ = _____ ¢

4. She gives you 3 quarters.
   How much change
   should you give back? _____ ¢ − _____ ¢ = _____ ¢

5. Brad has 1 .

   How many 🍪 s can he buy?

   _____

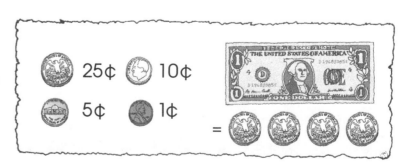

25¢ 10¢

5¢ 1¢ =

Coin Values

A Cool Pool

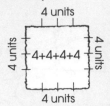

The perimeter is 16 units.

Swimming pools come in different shapes.
This swimming pool is a rectangle. It has four sides.
Count the units around the pool to find its perimeter.

SWIMMING POOL

Find the perimeter of each.

1. swimming pool _____

2. wading pool _____

3. sandbox _____

4. patio _____

5. Name the shape of the sandbox.

_____

_____

WADING POOL

Perimeter and Shapes

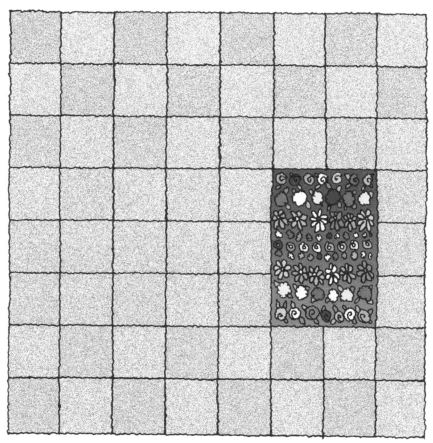

PATIO

SANDBOX

6. Circle the one with the greater
   perimeter.

   sandbox   wading pool

7. Draw two towels on the patio.
   Make a red one 3 units wide and 4
   units long. Make a green one 2 units wide
   and 5 units long. Find the perimeter of each towel.

   red _____

   green _____

Perimeter and Shapes

More Than One

To make more than one, add **s** to most nouns. Add **es** to nouns that end with **s**, **ss**, **ch**, **sh**, or **x**.

Study the pictures. Read the nouns.

pitcher

pitchers

peach

peaches

Make the noun in the ( ) name more than one. Then write the new word.

1. The children used three (box) to make a lemonade stand.

_____

2. Mother gave them some (lemon).

_____

3. She also gave them some (glass).

_____

4. They need ice (cube) to keep the lemonade cold.

_____

5. They also need (coin) to make change for customers.

_____

6. The children ate (sandwich) and drank lemonade.

_____

Who's in the Nest?

Help these math birds return to their answer nests!
Write their names in the nests below.

Al

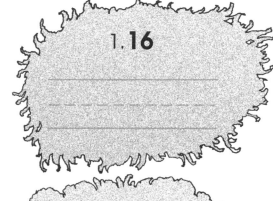

Bob

The number is 2
greater than 10 + 3.

The number is 1 less
than 2 tens + 8 ones.

Joe

The number is 4 less
than 4 + 0.

Sue

Ben

You say the number
if you count by twos.

The number is
5 less than 9 + 9.

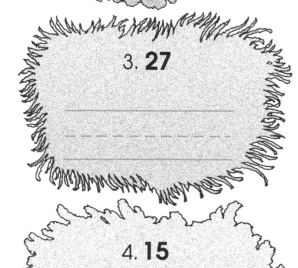

1. **16**

_____

_____

2. **13**

_____

_____

3. **27**

_____

_____

4. **15**

_____

_____

_____

5. Which bird does not have a nest? _____

Addition/Subtraction

Card Game

Use the numbers on the cards only once.

1. Find the greatest sum.

□ □

□

+ _____

_____

2. Find the least sum.

□ □

□

+ _____

_____

Use these cards. Write the greatest number
you can. Write the least number you can.

	Greatest Number	Least Number

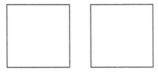

3. _____ _____

4. _____ _____

5. _____ _____

Place Value

Big Fish, Little Fish

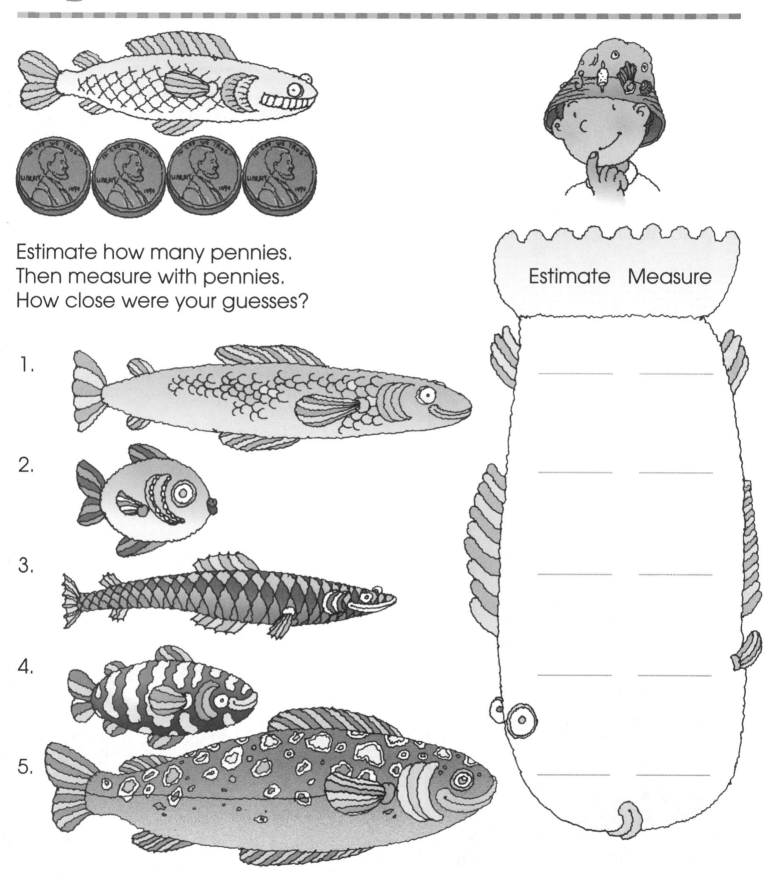

Estimate how many pennies.
Then measure with pennies.
How close were your guesses?

Estimate	Measure
1.	
2.	
3.	
4.	
5.	

Estimate Measures

On the Go

Answer the riddles about ways to travel.
Then circle the words in the puzzle.

1. What word rhymes with slip?

_____

_____

2. What word rhymes with star?

_____

_____

3. What word rhymes with rain?

_____

_____

4. What word rhymes with us?

_____

_____

5. What word rhymes with pet?

_____

_____

```
S  H  P  J  E  T  E  B
T  P  W  A  B  T  E  U
R  Z  S  H  I  P  T  L
A  T  R  I  L  C  B  N
I  C  L  B  C  A  U  I
N  A  I  U  A  C  A  R
B  U  L  S  M  U  R  P
```

Rhyming Words

Off We Go!

People get from here to there in different ways.
Look at the pictures. Write the words on the lines below.

Land

_____

_____

_____

_____

Water

_____

_____

_____

_____

Air

_____

_____

_____

_____

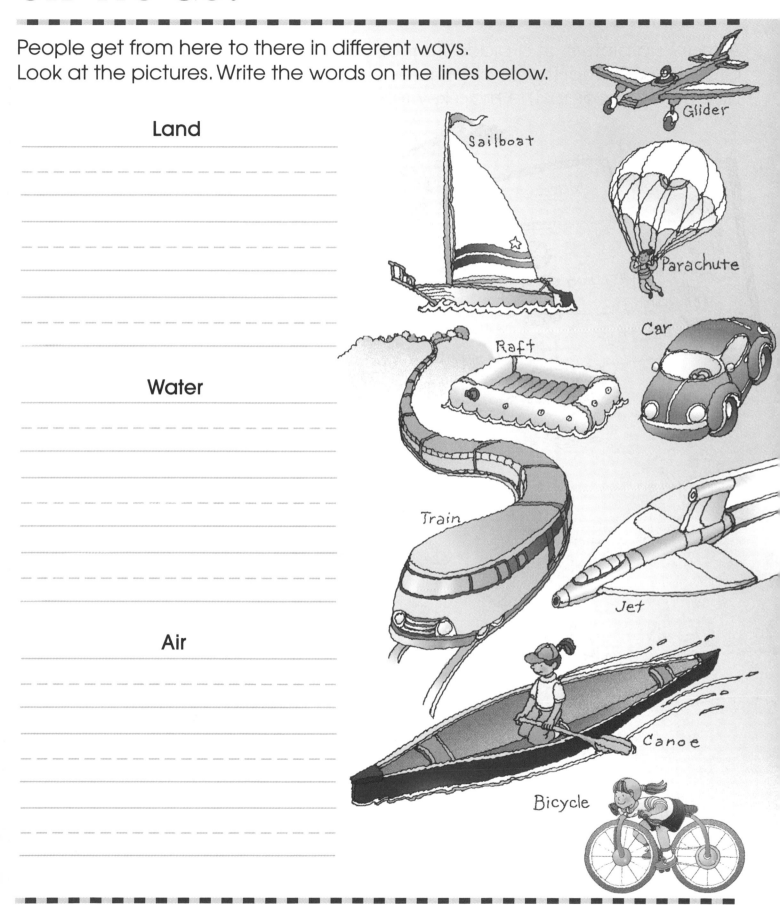

Glider

Sailboat

Parachute

Car

Raft

Train

Jet

Canoe

Bicycle

Transportation

Crow River Camp

A map is a picture of a place from above. This map shows Crow River Camp. The small pictures on the map stand for different places in the camp. The map key tells what the small pictures mean.

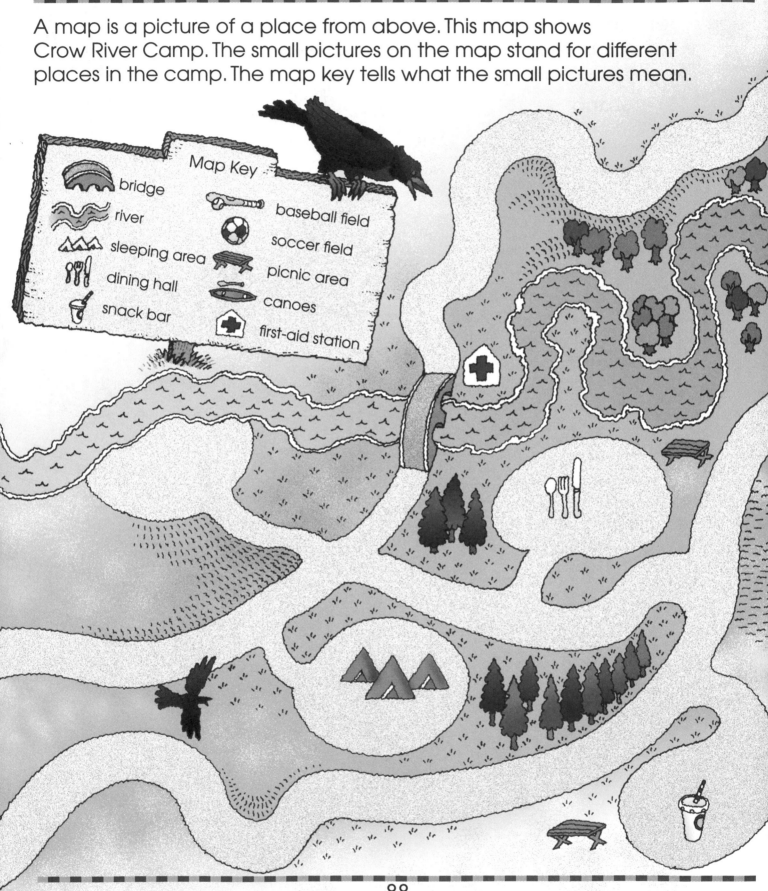

Map Key

bridge
river
sleeping area
dining hall
snack bar

baseball field
soccer field
picnic area
canoes
first-aid station

Map and Map Key

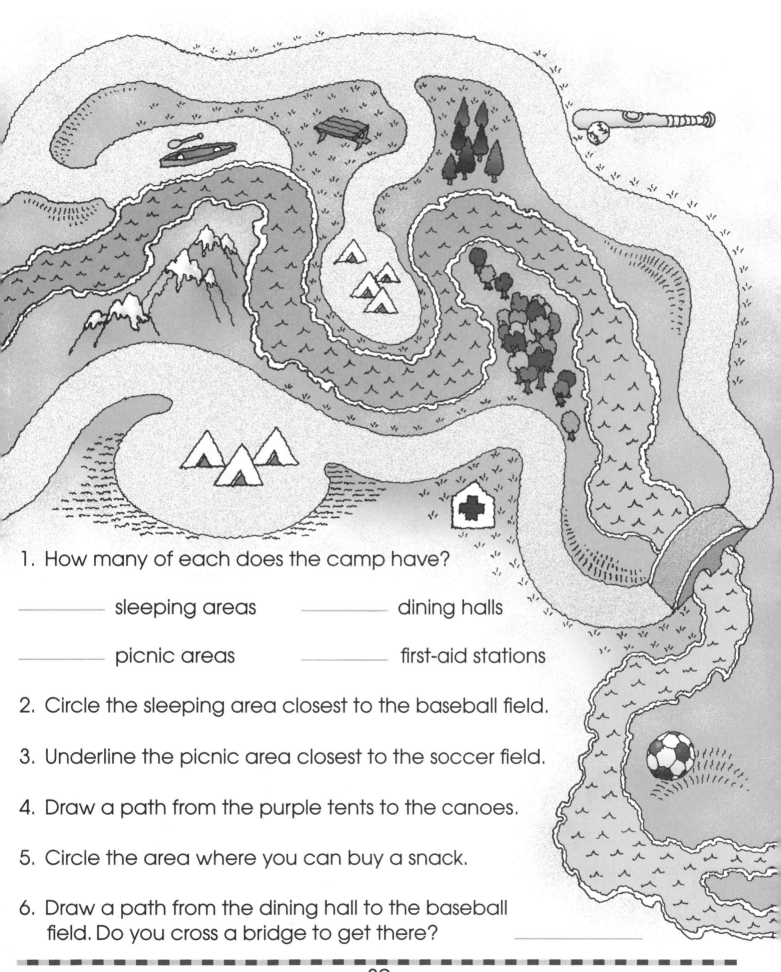

1. How many of each does the camp have?

_____ sleeping areas   _____ dining halls

_____ picnic areas   _____ first-aid stations

2. Circle the sleeping area closest to the baseball field.

3. Underline the picnic area closest to the soccer field.

4. Draw a path from the purple tents to the canoes.

5. Circle the area where you can buy a snack.

6. Draw a path from the dining hall to the baseball field. Do you cross a bridge to get there? _____

Map and Map Key

Bunkmates

ABC order is the order of the letters in the alphabet.
Use the first letters of words to put them in ABC order.

ant   **cat**   **pig**

The words *dig*, *dog*, and *day* begin with the same
first letter. Use their second letters to put them in
ABC order.

day   **dig**   **dog**

Put the names of these bunkmates in ABC order.

1. Peter, Matt, Jamie

_____ _____ _____

_____ _____ _____

2. Lucy, Tina, Beth

_____ _____ _____

_____ _____ _____

3. David, Drew, Doug

_____ _____ _____

_____ _____ _____

4. Amy, Abby, Anna

_____ _____ _____

_____ _____ _____

Tent Teams

Look at the numbers on each flag.
Write four number facts in each tent.

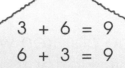

3,6,9

$3 + 6 = 9$
$6 + 3 = 9$
$9 - 3 = 6$
$9 - 6 = 3$

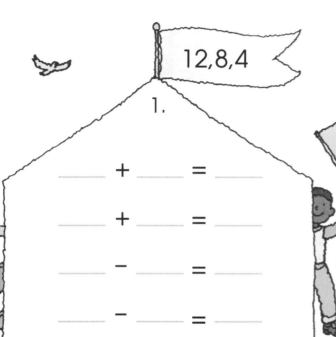

12,8,4

1.

___ + ___ = ___

___ + ___ = ___

___ - ___ = ___

___ - ___ = ___

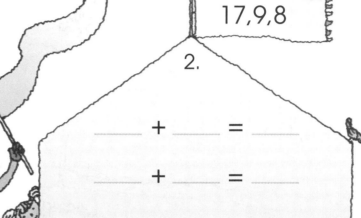

17,9,8

2.

___ + ___ = ___

___ + ___ = ___

___ - ___ = ___

___ - ___ = ___

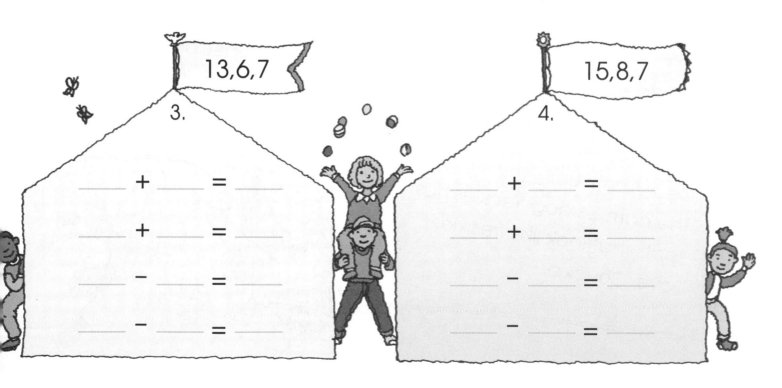

13,6,7

3.

___ + ___ = ___

___ + ___ = ___

___ - ___ = ___

___ - ___ = ___

15,8,7

4.

___ + ___ = ___

___ + ___ = ___

___ - ___ = ___

___ - ___ = ___

Fact Families

Postcards from Camp

Some children wrote postcards from camp. They forgot to use a capital letter to begin the name of a person, a pet, or a month. Find and circle each word that needs a capital letter.

Dear Mom,
Please pat my dog pat
and say hello to him for me.
Love, Tim

Dear Dad,
A lucky girl named penny
found a penny in the woods.
Love, Katie

Dear Grandma,
My best friend may come
and visit me in may.
Love, Jon

Dear Kelly,
Next march, people from my
camp will march in a parade.
Love, Carrie

Dear Aunt Sue,
The camp's dog freckles has
spots that look like freckles.
Love, Chuckie

92

Admission Is Free

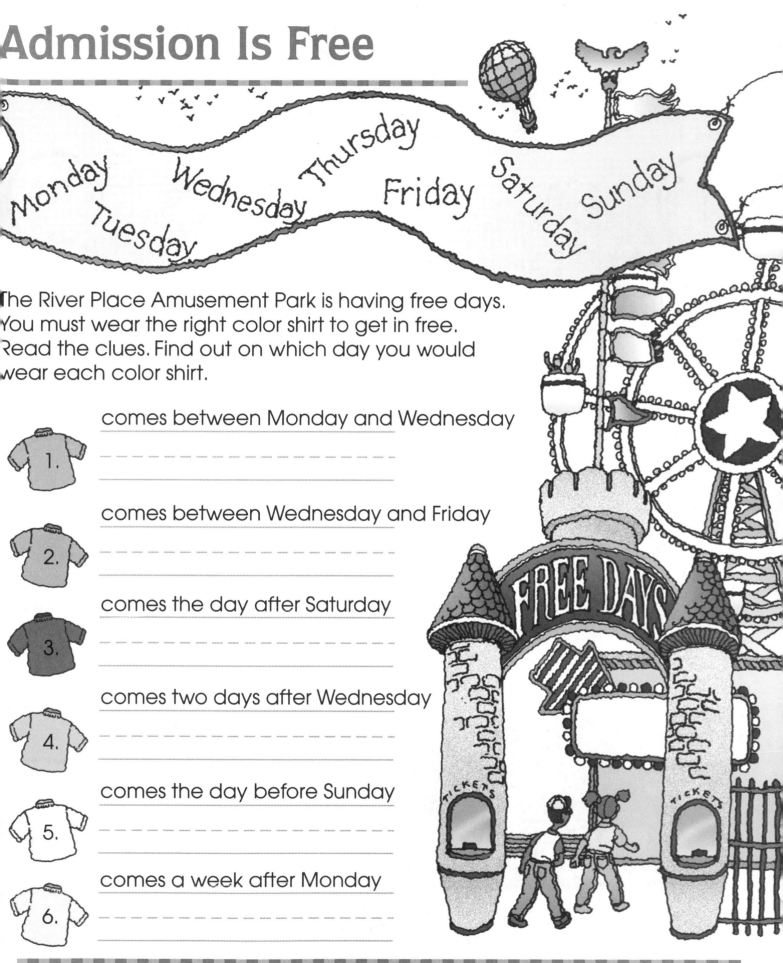

Monday Tuesday Wednesday Thursday Friday Saturday Sunday

The River Place Amusement Park is having free days.
You must wear the right color shirt to get in free.
Read the clues. Find out on which day you would
wear each color shirt.

1. comes between Monday and Wednesday

2. comes between Wednesday and Friday

3. comes the day after Saturday

4. comes two days after Wednesday

5. comes the day before Sunday

6. comes a week after Monday

Time Gone By

Answer each question.
Show the time on each clock.

Ann's family arrived at River Place Amusement Park at 11:30 A.M.
They ate lunch an hour later. What time did they eat lunch?

Ann's watch read 1:15 P.M. She and her family waited in line for a half
hour at the Haunted House. What time did they get in?

The trip through the Haunted House takes 20 minutes. If you go in
at 1:45 P.M., what time will you come out?

Elapsed Time

Clock Towers

River Place Amusement Park has two clock towers.
Characters come out at special times.
Write the time for each clock.
Draw the missing clock hands to complete the pattern.

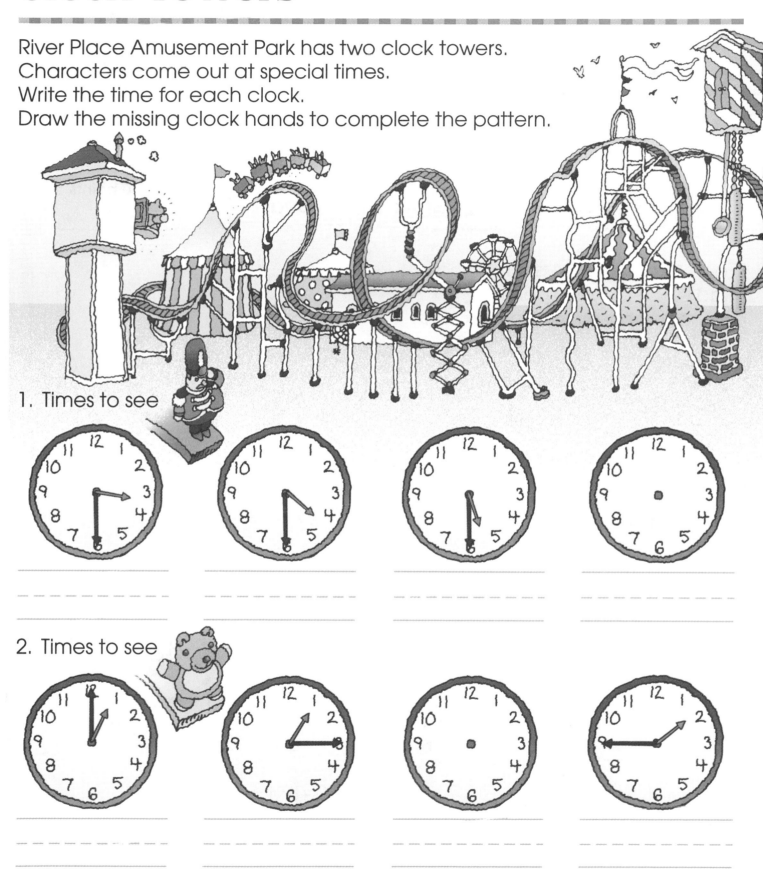

1. Times to see

_____   _____   _____   _____

2. Times to see

_____   _____   _____   _____

95

Ring Toss

| 11–14 points **Rag Doll** | 15–18 points **Baseball** | 19–22 points **Bear** | 23–30 points **Lion** |

Each player can toss three rings.
Add each player's points.
Name the prize each player wins.

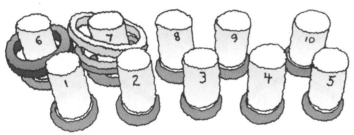

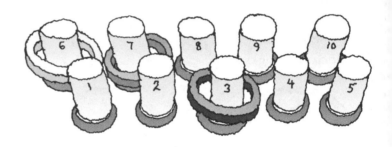

1. 7 + 7 + 6 = _____

prize _____

2. 6 + 7 + 3 = _____

prize _____

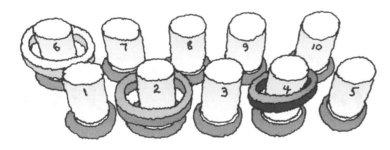

3. 6 + 2 + 4 = _____

prize _____

4. 10 + 9 + 5 = _____

prize _____

Addition

Light or Heavy?

Circle the one that is heavier in each pair.

Circle the one that is lighter in each pair.

Weight Comparison

Ice Cream Cones

The Camp Snack Bar sells ice cream cones.
What flavors of ice cream cones are liked best?
Count the tally marks in the table.

| = 1 vote ||||| = 5 votes

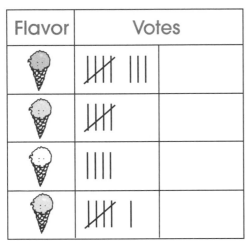

Flavor	Votes	
🍦	|||| |||	
🍦	||||	
🍦	||||	
🍦	||||		

1. How many like chocolate best? _____

2. How many like strawberry best? _____

3. How many like vanilla best? _____

4. How many like blue moon best? _____

Fill in the bar graph with the information from the table.

Votes for Favorite Flavor

	0	1	2	3	4	5	6	7	8	9	10
🍦											
🍦											
🍦											
🍦											

Number of Votes

Bar Graphs

Straw Shapes

Look at each set of straws.

Circle two shapes you can make with each set.

1.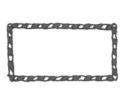

2.

3.

4.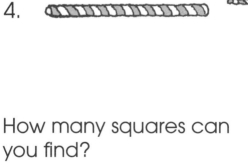

How many squares can you find?

_____ squares

Shapes

Water Animals

A **fact** can be proved.
   Fish live in water.
An **opinion** is what someone believes.
   Fish are nice.

Write *fact* or *opinion* after each sentence.

1. Most ocean animals are fish.

2. Fish get oxygen through gills.

3. Fish make good pets.

4. Whales and dolphins are not fish.

5. Everyone should eat fish.

6. Fish have backbones.

7. Ocean fish are better than river fish.

8. Fishing is a good sport.

Find the Way Home

Help the sea horse find its way home.
Start at 12 and count by 2s.

18	20	12	14	16	24	30	35	28	32
12	15	29	37	18	20	60	52	45	40
22	30	28	26	24	22	30	35	40	42
43	32	34	45	38	52	46	48	50	58
52	47	36	38	40	42	44	62	52	60
55	72	70	68	56	58	82	56	54	73
62	74	67	66	64	62	60	58	90	88
88	76	78	80	82	71	76	92	94	96
90	87	70	76	84	86	88	90	97	98
87	93	76	81	77	63	52	99	89	100

Welcome Home Dad!

Skip Counting by Twos

Nature Cycles

Most plants and animals live through cycles.
Here is the life cycle for a tree.

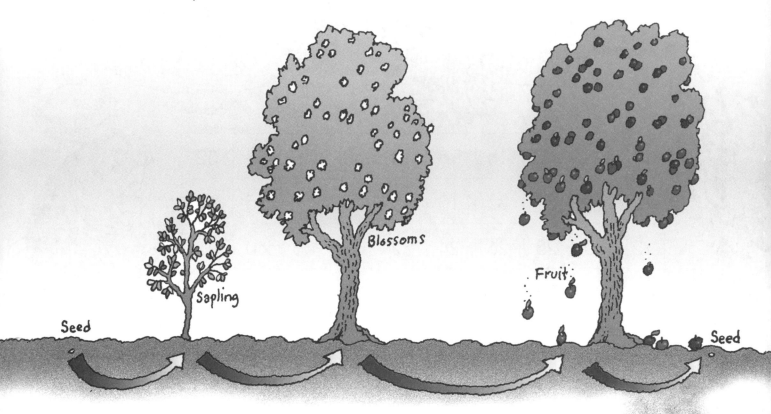

Seed Sapling Blossoms Fruit Seed

Write the missing word.

1. A tree begins as a _____.

2. Next, it becomes a _____.

3. A mature tree produces _____.

4. The blossoms become _____.

5. The fruit drops _____s.

Every butterfly goes through four
stages during its life cycle:

1. egg
2. larva (caterpillar)
3. pupa (chrysalis)
4. adult (butterfly)

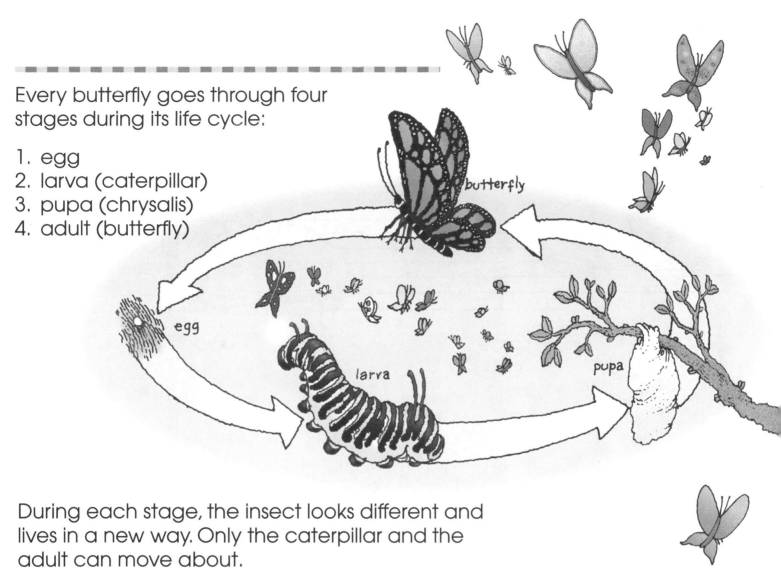

egg

larva

pupa

butterfly

During each stage, the insect looks different and
lives in a new way. Only the caterpillar and the
adult can move about.

Write the missing word.

1. A butterfly begins as an _____ .

2. The egg hatches into a _____ .

3. The caterpillar turns into a _____ .

4. A _____ breaks out of the pupa.

Butterfly Life Cycle

Bumper Cars

On the chart, write a word from a bumper car that means the same or opposite.

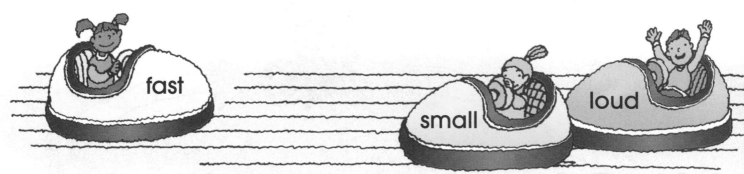

	same	opposite
glad		
noisy		
little		
quick		

Antonyms and Synonyms

Sound-alikes

Some words sound alike, but they have different spellings and meanings. Write the correct word to finish the sentences.

1. The _____ girls are going _____ town.
   to two   to two

2. They _____ their bikes on a bumpy _____ .
   rode road   rode road

3. The girls will meet _____ mother when they
                       there their

   get _____ .
       there their

4. They _____ she would bring them a _____ book.
   new knew   new knew

5. Mother said she would _____ the book _____
                          by buy   by buy

   lunchtime.

Camp Crafts

The campers are doing crafts.
They are making bracelets.

1. Steve has 10 beads on his string.
   Circle the fraction that tells what
   part of his bracelet is red.

   1/2   1/3   1/4

2. Pam has 9 beads on her string.
   Circle the fraction that tells what
   part of her bracelet is purple.

   1/2   1/3   1/4

3. Three children share 12 green
   beads equally. Circle how many
   each child has. Then circle the
   fraction that tells what part that is.

   1/2   1/3   1/4

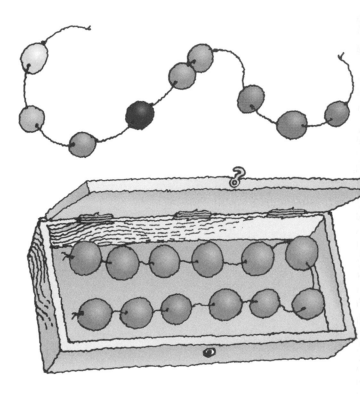

4. Color 2/5 of these beads red.

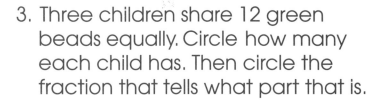

5. Color 3/4 of these beads blue.

Fractions

It's a Puzzle!

Look at the clues and solve the problems.
Write the answers in the puzzle.

ACROSS

A. 2 more than 8
B. 105, 110, 115
C. 19 + 5
D. 21 – 8
E. 9, 12, 15
F. 3 tens, 8 ones
G. 120 –15
H. 45 ¢ + 45 ¢
I. 40 – 27
J. 3 x 4

DOWN

A. 200 – 50
B. 20 – 9
C. 2 hundreds, 4 tens, 8 ones
D. 27 – 15
E. 2 x 9
F. 5 x 7
G. one dozen
H. $12.04 – $3.02

Math Puzzle

A Summer Album

This is an album of summer fun.
Write captions for the pictures.
Tell what you like about each.

Activities to Share

Language Arts

🍃 **Your Child—the Writer**

Encourage your child to make up a story or recount an experience. As the "official recorder," write down your child's words. After the piece is finished, examine it together. Does your child want to change anything? Post the dictation on the refrigerator door where you and your child can reread it.

🍃 **Develop Listening Skills**

After watching a TV program or a movie, encourage your child to tell you what happened. These discussions will help develop your child's abilities to listen carefully and speak fluently.

🍃 **It's in the Journal**

Give your child the opportunity to write in his or her very own journal, perhaps a notebook for which your child draws a special cover. Tell your child that the journal may include pictures with sentences that accompany them, stories, or descriptions of daily events.

🍃 **Taste the Stories**

When you and your child read a book that involves food as part of the plot, sample the food mentioned in the story. For example, if you read Maurice Sendak's **Chicken Soup with Rice** or Beatrix Potter's **Peter Rabbit**, follow up by making chicken soup with rice or munching on garden vegetables.

🍃 **Read the Signs**

Have your child read road signs and the names of various businesses as you travel in your car. At the grocery store, encourage your child to read the signs to figure out which foods are found in the various aisles. Your child may also enjoy reading the backs of cereal boxes and milk cartons.

🍃 **Read to Others**

If your child has a little brother or sister or if there is a younger child in the neighborhood, encourage your child to read to him or her. Provide an easy-to-read book, and let your child share the book with the younger child. Sharing books this way will build the child's confidence as a reader as well as demonstrate the rewards of sharing.

🍃 **Read, Read, Read!**

Reading to your child frequently is the best way to make sure your child will be a competent reader—and one who enjoys reading. You may want to pick a special reading time during the day. Read all sorts of books, including nonfiction and poetry. From time to time, encourage your child to predict what a book will be about from its title and illustrations. Occasionally, discuss a book briefly after you read it.

Activities to Share

Fiction

Here are some books you and your child may enjoy. They have themes and concepts compatible with **Second Grade Scholar**.

Aylesworth, Jim. **Hush Up!** Holt, 1980. It all starts when a horsefly bites a mule. Find out what happens.

Conover, Chris. **Froggie Went A-Courting**. Farrar, Straus & Giroux, 1986. This is a fun-to-sing version of the traditional folk song.

Kalan, Robert. **Jump, Frog, Jump!** Greenwillow, 1981.

Lobel, Arnold. **Frog and Toad Are Friends**. Harper, 1970.

McCloskey, Robert. **Make Way for Ducklings**. Viking, 1941. In this classic story, a mallard family decides to live in busy Boston.

Van Rynbach, Iris. **The Soup Stone**. Greenwillow, 1988. This folktale tells what people can accomplish if they work together.

Yolen, Jane. **Owl Moon**. Philomel, 1987. A father and child find an owl in the night woods.

Nonfiction

Cole, Joanna. **A Frog's Body**. Morrow, 1980.

Hornblow, Leonora. **Birds Do the Strangest Things**. Random House, 1965.

Wildsmith, Brian. **Birds**. Oxford, 1967.

 Science

The Science of Sound

Help your child to make a musical instrument by wrapping a rubber band around a coffee can. Let the child pluck the rubber band and discover what happens. Your child will notice that the rubber band moves, or **vibrates**, to make a sound. Have your child experiment with six thick rubber bands stretched around a plastic box to make a "guitar." Let your child tune the guitar by tightening some of the rubber bands on the edge of the box to make different notes. Do the tightly stretched rubber bands make higher or lower notes than the untightened ones? Have your child form a theory about why the more tightly stretched rubber bands make higher notes.

Shadow Fun

Help your child make puppets by cutting outlines of people and animals out of cardboard or construction paper. Tape the puppets onto popsicle sticks or craft sticks. Hang a sheet across a doorway as a screen. You and your child stand with flashlights on one side of the sheet. Turn out the lights. Have your child hold the puppets while you shine the flashlights on them to cast a shadow on the sheet. Move the flashlights. Have your child observe that the nearer the flashlight is to the puppet, the bigger the puppet becomes. This is because as the flashlight gets nearer the puppet, the puppet blocks more light and creates a bigger shadow.

Experiment with Water

Fill two jars with water to the same level. Put the lid on one jar and leave the lid off the other. Check the jars in a few days. The jar without the lid should contain less water. Where did the water go? Let your child think about it. The only place the water could have gone was into the air. The water made the air moister.

Now have your child fill a jar with ice water. Check the jar about half an hour later. What has happened? Water drops have gathered on the outside of the glass. Where did the water drops come from? If your child guesses the air, he or she is correct. The cold air near the water glass couldn't hold as much water as warm air, so water dropped out of the air and formed on the glass.

Collections

Your child can collect interesting things from a backyard, park, or playground. Leaf collections can be made in the summer or fall. Have your child hunt for as many different kinds of leaves as possible. Tape the leaves onto pieces of paper, stack the sheets in a pile, and weight the pile with several heavy books. Consult guidebooks to identify the trees from which the leaves came.

Your child can increase his or her knowledge of geology by making a rock collection. He or she can begin by collecting small rocks and stones in the neighborhood. As you travel, your child can be on the lookout for interesting rocks, too.

Children enjoy collecting seeds. The seeds can be from produce such as watermelons, cantaloupes, apples, and peaches. You may also explore your backyard or the local park to find seeds. Your child may want to let the seeds dry, glue them to cardboard, and label them, or your child may decide to germinate and plant some of the seeds to see what kind of plant grows.

Read More About It

Here are some science books your child may enjoy. They explore some themes and concepts in this book.

Cole, Joanna. **The Magic Schoolbus at the Waterworks**. Scholastic, 1986. Ms. Frizzle's class learns about the water cycle by becoming raindrops.

Heller, Ruth. **Birds Aren't the Only Ones**. Grosset & Dunlap, 1981. Here's a chance to find out about eggs and egg layers.

Kramer, Stephen P. **How to Think Like a Scientist**. Crowell, 1987. A practical book that encourages your child to use the scientific method.

Spier, Peter. **Peter Spier's Rain**. Doubleday, 1982. Two children watch the sequence of a storm in this wordless book.

Wilkes, Angela, and David Mostyn. **Simple Science**. Usborne, 1983. This book is filled with simple, fun experiments you and your child can perform.

Activities to Share

Activities to Share

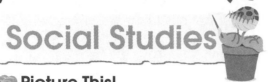

Social Studies

👄 Picture This!

Help your child take photographs of familiar places in your neighborhood, such as the grocery store, post office, gas station, fire station, and a friend's house. After the photos are printed, help your child glue them on a sheet of butcher paper to make a map of your neighborhood.

👄 Community Workers

Talk with your child about community workers, such as checkout clerks, police officers, doctors, and teachers. Help your child set up an interview with one of these people. Let your child ask the person questions about his or her job and help the child write or tape record the answers. When you return home, have your child draw a picture of the worker and write a sentence that explains what the worker does. Encourage your child to give the worker the picture as a thank-you gift for the interview.

👄 Family Storytelling Quilt

Tell your child a story about a family member. After you tell the story, have your child draw a portrait of that person. Hang the picture on your child's bedroom wall. As an ongoing activity, have your child draw a picture of other family members as you tell stories about them. Your child can tape the pictures together on the wall to make a family storytelling quilt. Encourage your child to retell the stories.

👄 Eating History

Let your child help you read recipes and prepare a dish for which your area of the country is noted. For example, if you live by the water, you might prepare fish or other seafood; if you live in Iowa, you might cook a corn dish; if you live in California or Texas, you might choose tacos. As you cook with your child, discuss the importance of the food to your area and to your family.

👄 Read More About It

Here are some social studies books your child may enjoy that expand on some of the social studies topics in **Second Grade Scholar**.

Aardema, Verna. **Bringing the Rain to Kapiti Plain**. Dial, 1981. This entertaining African folktale has lots of information about Africa.

Hall, Donald. **Ox-Cart Man**. Viking, 1979. A farmer loads his produce from the farm onto an ox cart. He sells his produce in Portsmouth and heads back to the farm.

Lyon, David. **The Runaway Duck**. Lothrop, Lee & Shepard, 1985. A toy duck is in for the ride of its life when it rolls away accidentally. A map shows where the duck goes.

Martin, Charles. **Island Rescue**. Greenwillow, 1985. In this adventure, the island is shown as a habitat in which people and animals are seen through a child's eyes.

Williams, Vera B. **Three Days on a River in a Red Canoe**. Greenwillow, 1981. Children tell about their adventure on their canoe trip using maps.

Mathematics

The National Council of Teachers of Mathematics (NCTM) has developed the Curriculum and Evaluation Standards for School Mathematics to recommend appropriate mathematical preparation for grades K-12. These standards specify that the mathematics curriculum should emphasize problem solving, use reasoning skills, communicate about mathematics, and make connections among math topics and other subjects. It also specifies that children should learn to value mathematics and become confident in their own abilities. The NCTM advises that children have hands-on and varied experiences; use manipulatives, calculators and computers; and work in pairs or cooperative groups.

There are many ways you can help your child accomplish the NCTM goals at home. Here are some suggestions.

Follow Up the Lessons

Follow up each math lesson with similar types of activities. Help your child retain major mathematical concepts and skills by asking similar questions or thinking of similar problems. Urge him or her to talk about the problems to develop communication skills. Ask how school lessons are similar to these activities.

Math Journal

Use a notebook as a math journal. Have your child record math vocabulary words as they appear in the lessons. Review these words from time to time by talking about them and suggesting your child write about them. Have your child record interesting problems and puzzles. Ask the child to write about ways math is used every day at home, in stores, or in the neighborhood. The math journal can be taken on trips for your child to make entries about numbers on signs or buildings, record license plate numbers or time and temperature, and list ways a number can be written (10 = 4 + 6, 3 + 3 + 2 + 2, and so on). Many Try It! activities can be done in the math journal.

Math Every Day

Nurture your child's curiosity by asking a math question every day. Ask your child to help you figure out an answer to a real-life problem, such as finding the best buy or measuring something. Ask him or her about the shapes in nature and man-made things, such as boxes or buildings. Plan periodic hunts for mathematics in the home, at an event, or in the park. Involve other members of the family.

Develop Problem Solvers

Have counters handy for your child to figure out computational problems if addition or multiplication facts are not recalled easily. Use common objects, such as coins, straws, or buttons. Also help your child realize that there may be many ways to solve a problem and that some problems have more than one solution. When your child makes a mistake, analyze the approach and information used.

Activities to Share

Aylesworth, Jim. **Old Black Fly**. Henry Holt and Company, Inc., 1992. A fabulous picture book using alphabetical order and rhyme to tell about the chaos a black fly causes one hot summer day.

Coates, Grace Dávila, and Jean Kerr Stenmark. **Family Math for Young Children**. The Regents of the University of California, 1997. A book filled with interesting and fun investigations, activities, and explorations that children and parents can do together.

Gibbons, Gail. **The Reasons for Seasons**. Holiday House, 1995. A simple illustrated explanation of what causes the seasons and why they continue to come again year after year.

Hall, Zoe. **The Apple Pie Tree**. The Blue Sky Press (Scholastic Inc.), 1996. Follows the changes in an apple tree through the seasons, showing how the tree plays an important part in the lives of some animals and children that depend upon it.

Math Matters! Grolier Educational, 1999. A series of books written for children focusing on 13 important math concepts. Titles include **Numbers, Adding, Subtracting, Multiplying, Dividing, Decimals, Fractions, Shape, Size, Tables and Charts, Grids and Graphs, Chance and Average, Mental Arithmetic**.

Murphy, Stuart J. **Lemonade for Sale**. MathStart Series. HarperCollins, 1998. Four children need some money to fix up their clubhouse, so they open a lemonade stand. Readers are introduced to the concept of graphing as the children track their sales on a simple bar graph, showing the number of cups sold each day. Other titles in the series include **Too Many Kangaroo Things to Do, Divide and Ride,** and **Betcha**.

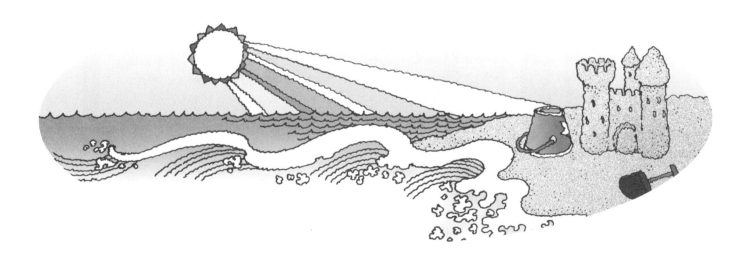

Activities to Share

Ross, Kathy. **Crafts to Make in the Summer**. The Millbrook Press, 1999. Contains directions for 29 easy-to-make projects using materials that are easy to find in the summertime.

School Zone Interactive. **On-Track Software**. These electronic workbooks provide proven School Zone workbooks in an exciting interactive format. The easy-to-use software provides audio guidance, tracks each child's progress, and features fun arcade games.

School Zone Publishing. **Second Grade Enrichment**. Extend your child's understanding of math, science, social studies, and language arts. This colorful workbook will capture your child's curiosity with entertaining activities that spark creativity and critical thinking.

Steiner, Joan. **Look-Alikes**. Little, Brown, 1998. Parents and children alike will enjoy puzzling over the illustrations in this book, looking for more than 1,000 everyday objects cleverly hidden in plain sight.

Teague, Mark. **How I Spent My Summer Vacation**. Crown Publishers, 1995. On his summer vacation, Wallace Bleff heads out West to visit his aunt but is captured by cowboys along the way.

Teague, Mark. **The Lost and Found**. Scholastic Press, 1998. Imaginative tale of Wendell, Floyd, and Mona, who find adventure when they get lost in their school lost and found.

The United States Mint has a special Web site just for kids. Visit **www.usmint.gov/kids** to find out how money is made, the history of U.S. money, and more.

Your child can see pictures of antique postcards and stamps at the Web site for the Smithsonian National Postal Museum. Visit **www.si.edu/postal** for on-line exhibits, recent acquisitions, and collection highlights.

Activities to Share

Summer Riddles

Encourage your child to think about summer—its weather, plants, activities, and so on. Then take turns making up riddles about summer. For example, "I'm a summer flower. I have thorns. What am I?" Your riddles may be oral or written. If you write them, help your child use correct capitalization and punctuation. This activity will also reinforce listening skills.

Story Time

Provide frequent opportunities for your child to read throughout the summer months. You may want to have your child take part in a summer reading program at your local library. Help your child make and complete story maps about favorite books. Then have your child use the maps to summarize the books for you. A story map should be a chart with the following headings: Title, Author, Setting, Characters, Events.

Summertime

Challenge your child to see how many words he or she can find in the word *summertime*. You may want to post a large sheet of paper on the refrigerator or on a wall and invite your child to keep an ongoing list for several weeks. Encourage your child to check the spelling of words in a dictionary.

Picnic Words

Plan a picnic and ask your child to help you make a list of things you will need. After you have written the list, have your child identify the words that are nouns (plates) and the words that are adjectives (big). Then invite your child to add one or more adjectives to describe each noun. For example: old blanket; cheese sandwiches; big, red apples; cold, sour lemonade.

A Verb Game

Play a game in which family members take turns acting out verbs for each other to guess. Each verb must tell something that people like to do in the summer. Verbs might include swim, read, hit (a baseball), run, ride (a bike). Whoever guesses the correct verb first takes the next turn.

Sensing Summer

Invite your child to write a poem or a descriptive paragraph about summer using words that appeal to the senses. Tell your child that the poem or paragraph should describe what he or she sees, hears, smells, tastes, and feels in the summer. Encourage your child to brainstorm a list of ideas and sensory words. Then tell your child to choose the ones he or she likes best and use them to write the poem.

Activities to Share

Science

Watch for Animals
Take walks with your child throughout the summer to look for animals in nature. Have your child write in a notebook the names of the animals he or she sees. Reinforce your child's knowledge of animal groups by having him or her record the animals under appropriate headings: insects, birds, mammals, fish, amphibians, reptiles. Discuss the characteristics of animals in each group.

Safe Colors
Discuss the concept of camouflage with your child. Explain how color protects some animals because they match the background and their enemies cannot see them. Look for insects, birds, lizards, snakes, and toads hiding in the vegetation of summer: in the grass, among flowers, on branches, in leaves, or on tree trunks. Some butterflies, for example, have underwings that look like bark.

A Leaf Guidebook
Your child might enjoy collecting leaves from various trees in your neighborhood. Help your child identify the trees and put together "A Leaf Guidebook." Discuss the different kinds of leaves, simple leaf and compound leaf, and have your child arrange the leaves in the book according to type. If possible, include seedpods (fruit) in the book as well.

Plant Cycle
Demonstrate the life cycle of a plant to your child with a garden in a box. At the beginning of the summer, plant flower seeds in a flower box. Encourage your child to observe the plants as they grow and to note each phase of a plant's life. Help your child draw a labeled diagram of the life cycle of a plant. Use labels such as seed, seedling, leaves, bud, flower, new seeds, and wilting.

Moon Chart
Talk with your child about the different phases of the moon. Encourage him or her to observe the moon over the summer and record its phases. You may wish to compare your child's observations to a calendar that notes moon phases. Help your child make a "Moon Chart." Discuss the moon cycle, pointing out how the phases repeat.

Health Checklist
Help your child create a list of things he or she can do each day to stay healthy. The list might include such items as wash hands, eat a balanced diet, brush teeth, get fresh air, exercise, and get a good night's sleep. Encourage your child to check off what he or she remembers to do each day. You may wish to draw a happy face or put a sticker on the chart to acknowledge a "healthy week."

Activities to Share

Social Studies

Time Lines of Our Lives
Help your child make a time line of his or her life. Talk about important events and dates to include, such as when he or she was born, walked, talked, started preschool, started first grade, and started second grade. Make a simple time line of important events in your life and share it with your child. You may wish to draw your time lines outside on a pleasant summer day, writing with chalk on a driveway or sidewalk.

Making a Map
Have your child make a map of one section of your town or city. Help your child take notes during a walk around this area. Encourage your child to notice the streets; kinds of buildings (stores, restaurants, public buildings); and natural areas (parks, flowers, ponds, lakes). As your child works on the map, remind him or her to label the streets and create a key with symbols for the different kinds of things shown on the map.

Talk about Talking
Introduce your child to the history of the telephone. Talk about today's phones, and have your child find pictures of them in magazines and catalogs: push-button phones, cordless phones, cell phones, car phones, novelty phones. Then look in an encyclopedia together to see what phones were like in the past: dial phones, phones with no dials. Discuss how they are different from today's phones and how they are the same.

What Came Before?
"What Came Before?" is a card game you can play with your child during summer outings. Each player, in turn, takes a card, reads the invention, and then tells what came before it. Players get 1 point for each thing they name. Prepare several game cards by writing a modern invention on each one. Sample cards and answers include microwave oven (stove, fire), computer (typewriter, pencil), jet airplane (train, horse), TV (radio, newspaper).

Summer Trips
Point out to your child that many people take vacation trips during the summer. Explain that people go to outdoor places in different parts of America. Invite your child to make a "Travel Book" of these places by cutting out pictures from magazines. Have your child find examples of various landforms and bodies of water. Help him or her label pictures with geographical terms: mountains, plains, desert, island, peninsula, ocean, lake, and river.

My Park of the Future
Tell your child to think about an amusement park he or she has visited or seen on TV. Ask your child what he or she liked about the park. Then encourage your child to use his or her imagination and design a perfect amusement park of the future. Have your child create a name for the park, draw a plan of it, and tell you why it is a perfect amusement park.

Activities to Share

Activities to Share

Mathematics

Math at the Store

Take your child shopping with you to the grocery store or drugstore. Encourage your child to read the price stickers of items under $5.00. Then name an amount of money and ask your child if it is enough money to buy the item. For example, if a pair of sunglasses costs $2.79, ask "Is two dollars and one quarter enough money to buy the sunglasses? Is three dollars enough?"

Math on the Street

Walk along a neighborhood street with your child and play "I Spy a 3-D Shape." The winner is the first person to find each of these shapes: sphere, cylinder, cone, cube, and rectangular prism. You may see the shapes in balls, streetlight globes, trash cans, fence posts, bird feeders, watering cans, ice cream cones, road-construction cones, birdhouses, doghouses, or cardboard boxes.

Math in the Kitchen

Invite your child to help you prepare individual fruit salads for members of your family. Give your child the opportunity to use fractions as both of you arrange fruits on each plate. Cut fruits into halves and fourths and have your child name the fractional parts. Encourage your child to divide fruits such as grapes, cherries, and strawberries into equal groups.

Beach Math

Use a visit to the beach to make up addition and subtraction problems for your child to solve. For example, ask your child to collect 18 shells, subtract the number that are pink, then tell you how many shells are left. You could make sand animals together, keeping track of how many pails of sand you use for each animal. Then have your child figure out how many pails of sand you used altogether.

Holiday Math

Have your child make a crepe-paper flag to decorate for Flag Day or the Fourth of July. Help your child draw the flag on a large sheet of paper, measure the length of each stripe, and figure out how much red and white paper you will need to buy. Then brainstorm ideas to determine how much blue paper you will need.

Math and Summer Activities

Encourage your child to make a schedule of things he or she will do on one upcoming busy day. Discuss that a schedule includes the name of each activity and the time each activity begins. Have your child read the finished schedule and tell you how long each activity will take. At the end of the day, compare your child's estimates to the actual time required for each activity.

Answers

Page 2

1. teacher
2. parents
3. guide
4. visitors
5. Sentence will vary.

Page 3

6. carrying
7. climbs
8. starts
9. wave
10. Sentence will vary.

Pages 4–5

1. See map.
2. four
3. two
4. two
5. Places include grocery stores, parks, malls, and schools.

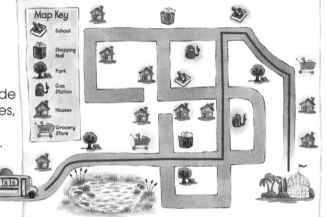

Page 6

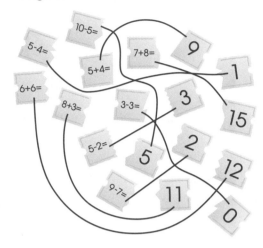

Page 7

1. There's, there + is
2. I'm, I + am
3. Here's, here + is
4. We'll, we + will or I'll, I + will
5. I'll, I + will or We'll, we + will
6. Let's, let + us

Page 8

Page 9

1. fact
2. fact
3. opinion
4. fact
5. opinion
6. opinion
7. opinion
8. fact

Page 10

$$\begin{array}{c} p \\ 9 \\ +7 \\ \hline 16 \end{array}$$ 1.

$$\begin{array}{c} e \\ 6 \\ +5 \\ \hline 11 \end{array}$$ 2.

$$\begin{array}{c} n \\ 7 \\ +6 \\ \hline 13 \end{array}$$ 3.

$$\begin{array}{c} s \\ 8 \\ +7 \\ \hline 15 \end{array}$$ 4.

$$\begin{array}{c} H \\ 9 \\ +8 \\ \hline 17 \end{array}$$ 5.

$$\begin{array}{c} g \\ 8 \\ +4 \\ \hline 12 \end{array}$$ 6.

$$\begin{array}{c} c \\ 5 \\ +4 \\ \hline 9 \end{array}$$ 7.

$$\begin{array}{c} r \\ 8 \\ +6 \\ \hline 14 \end{array}$$ 8.

$$\begin{array}{c} h \\ 6 \\ +4 \\ \hline 10 \end{array}$$ 9.

$$\begin{array}{c} n \\ 8 \\ +5 \\ \hline 13 \end{array}$$ 10.

$$\begin{array}{c} i \\ 6 \\ +2 \\ \hline 8 \end{array}$$ 11.

Answer: He's chirping.

Page 11

Page 12

1. plastic
2. metal
3. paper
4. glass
5. paper
6. plastic

Answers

Page 13

The other half of each bug should be drawn. Subtraction problems will vary, but differences should be the same on each half.

Example:

Pages 16–17

2. <u>butterflies</u> are in<u>s</u>ect<u>s</u><u>⊙</u>

3. <u>there</u> are many <u>k</u>ind<u>s</u> of butterflie<u>s</u><u>⊙</u>

4. <u>butterflies</u> live all over the world<u>⊙</u>

5. <u>they</u> help <u>f</u>lowers become fruit and seeds<u>⊙</u>

6. <u>most</u> butterflies <u>fl</u>y during the day<u>⊙</u>

7. Some butterflies <u>l</u>ive only a week or two<u>⊙</u>

8. <u>how</u> can they <u>d</u>efend themselves ?

9. <u>some</u> make themselves <u>s</u>tink<u>⊙</u>

10. <u>others</u> <u>t</u>aste bad <u>⊙</u>

11. <u>yuck</u> !

12. <u>who</u> wants to be a butterfly ?

Page 21

1. green + houses
2. rain + forest
3. Every + one
4. note + books
5. back + packs
6. Some + one
7. Some + body

Page 14

Page 18

Page 19

1. lots	spots
2. grow	slow
3. plants	ants
4. bugs	slugs
5. blow	grow
6. tall	wall

Page 22

1. hind
2. smooth
3. water
4. plump
5. bumpy
6. land

Answer: a m p h i b i a n s

Page 15

Which number is five after?
25 <u>30</u>
50 <u>55</u>
80 <u>85</u>

Which number is five before?
<u>25</u> 30
<u>60</u> 65

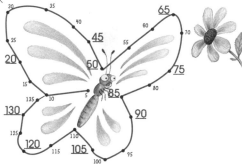

Page 20

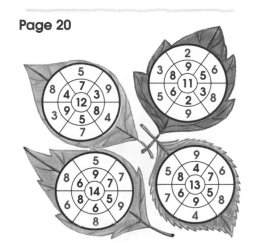

$\begin{array}{r}17\\-9\\\hline\end{array}$	$\begin{array}{r}16\\-8\\\hline\end{array}$	$\begin{array}{r}17\\-8\\\hline\end{array}$
1. 8	2. 8	3. 9
$\begin{array}{r}16\\-9\\\hline\end{array}$	$\begin{array}{r}15\\-8\\\hline\end{array}$	$\begin{array}{r}14\\-9\\\hline\end{array}$
4. 7	5. 7	6. 5

Page 23

Answers

Answers

Pages 24–25

1. a kind of bird
2. too many ants
3. Quail came to live in the garden.
4. faster
5. Most children will write that bamboo grows taller.
6. Bamboo is used for houses, furniture, and other necessary things.

Page 29

Children should have drawn blossoms on cactuses 2, 3, 5, 6, and 7.

Page 33

B Martin Luther King Day, January 20

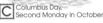
C Columbus Day, Second Monday in October

E Valentine's Day, February 14

D New Year's Day, January 1

A Independence Day, July 4

Page 26

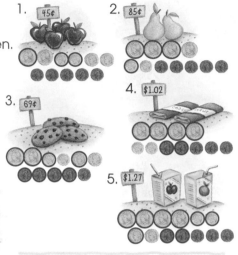

Page 30

1. 25, 8, 15, 58, 36
2. Answer should include the word *cactus*.

Page 31

_4_ **Mosses and Ferns**
by Eugenia Charles

_3_ **How Plants Grow**
by M. E. Patinkin

_1_ **Amazing Seeds**
by Janice Carson

_5_ **Plant Kingdoms**
by Alice Addams

_6_ **Wildflowers of the Midwest**
by Henry Spinella

_2_ **First Seeds, Then Plants**
by Gary Grove

Pages 34–35

Tropical Garden

rectangle

triangle

square

Page 27

1. water   2. trees
3. oil   4. fish
5. water   6. trees

Page 28

10:45   2:15

12:30   3:05

1:30   11:00

Page 32

1. May   October
   January   July
   March   September

2. September   April
   December   August
   June   February

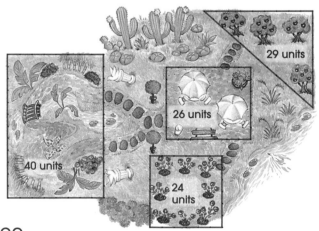

29 units

26 units

24 units

40 units

Answers

Page 36

gas

gas

liquid

solid

gas
liquid

solid

Page 37

1. 3/4   2. 1/4   3. 1/2   4. 4/6

5. 6/8   6. 2/3   7. 5/6

Page 39

1. seeds
2. dandelions
3. trees
4. coconuts
5. classes
6. buses
7. wishes
8. teaches

Page 40

1. Cactus
2. Poison Oak
3. Orange
4. Thistle
5. Rose

Page 38

3   2   5   1   4   6

Page 41

Wording of answers will vary.

1. The class has a snack.
2. Mrs. Cone's hat blows off.
3. Everyone puts on hats and scarves.
4. It gets warmer
5. A boy is missing
6. Someone gives star fruit to the class

Page 44

1. thermometer
2. tweezers
3. trowel
4. tape measure

Pages 42–43

Estimates will vary slightly.

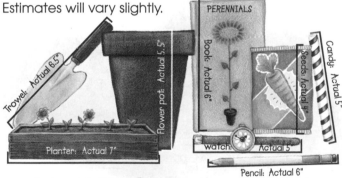

PERENNIALS

Trowel: Actual 6.5"

Flower pot: Actual 5.5"

Book: Actual 6"

Seeds: Actual 4"

Candy: Actual 5"

Planter: Actual 7"

Watch: Actual 5"

Earring: Actual 2"

Pencil: Actual 6"

5 inches
pencil & book, candy & watch

Page 45

1. producer

2. consumer

3. producer

4. consumer

5. producer

Page 46

LL	VA	OR	NI
29	18	15	17
+ 3	+ 5	+ 5	+ 9
32	23	20	26

A	S	CE	O
32	16	10	17
+ 8	+ 6	+14	+ 8
40	22	24	25

DU	CH	PR	ID
15	17	15	33
+16	+24	+15	+17
31	41	30	50

ORCHIDS PRODUCE VANILLA.

Answers

Answers

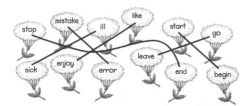

Page 47

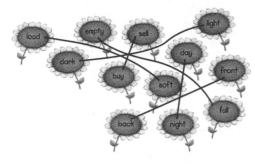

Page 48

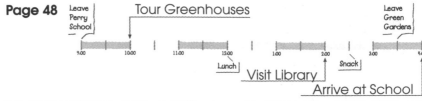

Tour Greenhouses
Leave Perry School
Leave Green Gardens
Lunch
Visit Library
Snack
Arrive at School

Page 49

1. yes
2. no
3. no
4. yes
5. no
6. yes

Page 50

1. 9
2. 6
3. $7 - 6 = 1$
4. $9 - 2 = 7$
5. $9 + 7 = 16$

Page 51

a. 2
b. 1
c. 1
d. 2

Page 54

1. Ms. Jones
2. Best wishes,
3. Mrs. Cone's class

Letter will vary, but all parts should be included and in the proper sequence.

Date

Greeting

Body

Closing

Signature

Page 53

Wording of answers will vary.

1. because his money was gone
2. because the bird was broken
3. because her purse was at the lost-and-found desk

Page 52

A.2	2			B.1	0	5
9		C.2	9	9		
6		2		D.1	7	
	E.1	2			5	
F.1	2		G.1	0	5	
8			5		H.2	8
I.8	5				3	
5				J.1	6	

Across
A. 22
B. 105
C. 29
D. 17
E. 12
F. 12
G. 105
H. 28
I. 85
J. 16

Down
A. 296
B. 19
C. 222
D. 15
E. 12
F. 18
G. 15
H. 236
I. 85

Answers

Page 56

1. Fall
2. Spring
3. Summer
4. Winter

Page 60

1. Father - Who
2. Mother - Who
3. Corn - What
4. Carrots - What

Pages 62-63

1. roots
2. leaves
3. seeds
4. stems
5. flowers
6. fruit
Drawing will vary.

Page 66

1. Amy plays in the sand.
2. Does Patty find a seashell?
3. Peter puts sand in his pail.
4. Brr! The water is cold.
   The water is cold. Brr!
5. Rex caught the ball.

Page 69

Page 57

Answers will vary.

hot   sunny
dry   humid

Pages 64-65

1. girls
2. ball
3. book
4. baby
5. Waves, rocks
   Sentences will vary.
6. pail, snail, tail
7. shell, bell, well

Page 67

1. 12 – 6 = 6
2. 15 – 7 = 8
3. 13 + 5 = 18
4. 8 + 8 = 16
5. 13 – 6 = 7

Page 70

Answers may vary.

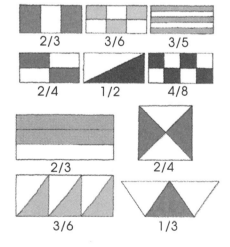

Pages 58-59

1. Winter
2. Summer
3. September, October, or November
4. 12
5. Month will vary.
6. Month will vary.
7. Month will vary.

Page 61

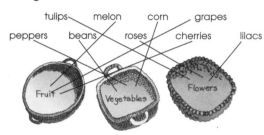

1. (carrot) orange (bean) (corn)
2. (hose) (rake) (shovel) plant
3. (leaf) green (stem) (root)
4. (lake) (pond) hill (river)
5. moon (day) (month) (year)
6. (fly) worm (bee) (mosquito)

Page 68

2/3   3/6   3/5

2/4   1/2   4/8

2/3   2/4

3/6   1/3

Answers

Page 71

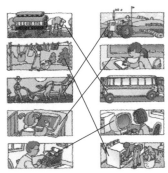

Checked items will vary.

Page 74

1. higher
2. highest
3. smoothest
4. faster
5. older
6. youngest

Page 78

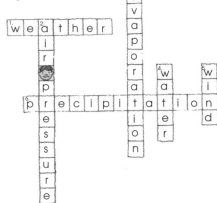

Page 72

1. February
2. July
3. October
4. December
5. Month will vary.
6. Name will vary.
7. Day will vary.
8. City or town will vary.

Page 75

Tracy and her family went <u>downtown</u> to watch the parade. They found a good spot between the <u>playground</u> and the <u>schoolhouse</u>. It was a hot day. They were standing <u>outside</u> in the sun for a long time. Luckily, the <u>fireworks</u> were at <u>nighttime</u>. So Tracy and her family cooled off in the evening.

1. down + town = downtown
2. play + ground = playground
3. school + house = schoolhouse
4. out + side = outside
5. fire + works = fireworks
6. night + time = nighttime

Page 79

1. 25¢ + 20¢ = 45¢
2. 50¢ – 45¢ = 5¢
3. 25¢ + 40¢ = 65¢
4. 75¢ – 65¢ = 10¢
5. He can buy 5 cookies.
   (20¢ x 5 = $1.00)

Page 73

1. tall, furry
2. Six, blue
3. pretty, shiny
4. big, loud

Page 77

Pages 80-81

1. 30 units
2. 16 units
3. 21 units
4. 32 units
5. triangle
6. sandbox
7. red: 14 units
   green: 14 units

Page 82

1. boxes
2. lemons
3. glasses
4. cubes
5. coins
6. sandwiches

Page 83

1. 16 - Ben
2. 13 - Sue
3. 27 - Bob
4. 15 - Al
5. Joe

Page 84

1. 8 5
   + 4
   ─────
     89

2. 3 6
   + 9
   ─────
     45

3. 941, 149
4. 872, 278
5. 653, 356

Page 85

1. 5.5
2. 2
3. 4.5
4. 2.5
5. 6.25

Estimates will vary.

Answers

Page 86

1. ship
2. car
3. train
4. bus
5. jet

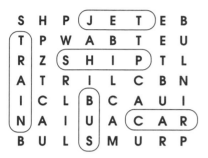

S	H	P	J	E	T	E	B
T	P	W	A	B	T	E	U
R	Z	S	H	I	P	T	L
A	T	R	I	L	C	B	N
I	C	L	B	C	A	U	I
N	A	I	U	A	C	A	R
B	U	L	S	M	U	R	P

Page 90

1. Jamie, Matt, Peter
2. Beth, Lucy, Tina
3. David, Doug, Drew
4. Abby, Amy, Anna

Page 93

1. Tuesday
2. Thursday
3. Sunday
4. Friday
5. Saturday
6. Monday

Page 95

1. 3:30 4:30 5:30 6:30

2. 1:00 1:15 1:30 1:45

Page 87

Land
bicycle
car
train

Water
canoe
raft
sailboat

Air
glider
jet
parachute

Page 91

1. 8 + 4 = 12
   4 + 8 = 12
   12 − 8 = 4
   12 − 4 = 8

2. 9 + 8 = 17
   8 + 9 = 17
   17 − 9 = 8
   17 − 8 = 9

3. 7 + 6 = 13
   6 + 7 = 13
   13 − 7 = 6
   13 − 6 = 7

4. 7 + 8 = 15
   8 + 7 = 15
   15 − 8 = 7
   15 − 7 = 8

Page 94

2:05

Page 96

1. 7 + 7 + 6 = 20
   Prize: Bear

2. 6 + 7 + 3 = 16
   Prize: Baseball

3. 6 + 2 + 4 = 12
   Prize: Rag Doll

4. 10 + 9 + 5 = 24
   Prize: Lion

Pages 88-89

1. 3 sleeping areas
   3 picnic areas
   1 dining hall
   2 first-aid stations

2. See blue circled area on map.
3. See underlined area on map.
4. See purple path on map.
5. See red circled area on map.
6. See green paths on map.
   There are two possible paths.
   Both paths cross a bridge.

Page 92

Dear Mom,
Please pat my dog (pat)
and say hello to him for me.
Love, Tim

Dear Dad,
A lucky girl named (penny)
found a penny in the woods.
Love, Katie

Dear Grandma,
My best friend (may) come
and visit me in (may.)
Love, Jon

Dear Kelly,
Next (march) people from my
camp will march in a parade.
Love, Carrie

Dear Aunt Sue,
The camp's dog (freckles) has
spots that look like freckles.
Love, Chuckie

Answers

Page 97

Page 98

1. 8
2. 5
3. 4
4. 6

Votes for Favorite Flavor										
🍦										
🍦										
🍦										
🍦										

0 1 2 3 4 5 6 7 8 9

Page 99

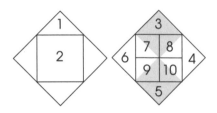

There are 10 squares.

Page 100

1. fact
2. fact
3. opinion
4. fact
5. opinion
6. fact
7. opinion
8. opinion

Page 101

18	20	12	14	16	24	30	35	28	32
12	15	29	37	18	20	60	52	45	40
22	30	28	26	24	22	30	35	40	42
43	32	34	45	38	52	46	48	50	58
52	47	36	38	40	42	44	62	52	60
55	72	70	68	56	58	82	56	54	73
62	74	67	66	64	62	60	58	90	88
88	76	78	80	82	71	76	92	94	96
90	87	70	76	84	86	88	90	97	98
87	93	76	81	77	63	52	99	89	100

Page 102

1. seed
2. sapling
3. blossoms
4. fruit
5. seed (seeds)

Page 103

1. egg
2. larva
3. pupa
4. butterfly

Page 104

glad - happy, sad
noisy - loud, quiet
little - small, big
quick - fast, slow

Page 105

1. two, to
2. rode, road
3. their, there
4. knew, new
5. buy, by

Page 106

1. 1/2
2. 1/3
3. 1/3

4.

2/5 = 4/10 (color in 4 beads)

5.

3/4 = 6/8
(color in 6 beads)

Page 107

A.1	0			B.1	2	0
5		C.2	4	1		
0		4			D.1	3
	E.1	8			2	
F.3	8		G.1	0	5	
5			2		H.9	0
	I.1	3			0	
					J.1	2

Page 108

Captions to pictures will vary.

   Second Grade Scholar 02463